# american nerd

*the story of my people*

benjamin nugent

SCRIBNER

*New York   London   Toronto   Sydney*

SCRIBNER
A Division of Simon & Schuster, Inc.
1230 Avenue of the Americas
New York, NY 10020

Copyright © 2008 by Benjamin Nugent

First Scribner hardcover edition May 2008

SCRIBNER and design are trademarks of
Macmillan Library Reference USA, Inc., used under license
by Simon & Schuster, the publisher of this work.

For information about special discounts for bulk
purchases, please contact Simon & Schuster Special Sales at
1-800-456-6798 or business@simonandschuster.com

Designed by Suet Y. Chong
Text set in Aldine 401

Manufactured in the United States of America

10   9   8   7   6   5   4   3   2

Library of Congress Cataloging-in-Publication Data

ISBN-13: 978-0-7432-8801-9
ISBN-10: 0-7432-8801-7

**Author's Note**
I don't make up, embellish, or in any other way fictionalize anything,
but I do change names to protect privacy.

for mindy

# contents

*part 3*

*part 1*

# a history of the nerd

Before I launch into a discussion of what a nerd is and where the idea of nerds comes from, I'd like to disclose that when I was eleven, I had a rich fantasy life in which I carried a glowing staff. On earth I ran to class under an L.L.Bean backpack erupting with books that I was too distracted by my medieval life to put in my locker, as I was pursued by an actual medieval-style warrior society of lacrosse players. When I saw them, I would blend with the crowd or run. They, in turn, established a pretty good Nugent impersonation: you bend forward at the waist to signify the burden of the swollen backpack and stick out your elbows, funky-chicken style, with your hands bunched into fists on your chest to signify the straps of the backpack clutched close to the body. Running through the halls with a backpack that was capable of doing real harm to others didn't do much to draw sympathy, so nobody raised serious objections when every once in a while somebody hit me in the crotch with a clarinet case or hockey stick. All of which is to say my journalistic objectivity with regard to my subject matter is seriously compromised. But I am trying my best.

That means I'm not writing a defense of nerds or a celebration of nerds or a polemic against the nerd stereotype. There is a rationale, I think, for despising the young me. I empathize with nerds and antinerds alike.

# what is a nerd?

As of this morning, Wikipedia states that "*nerd,* as a stereotypical or archetypal designation, refers to somebody who pursues intellectual interests at the expense of skills that are useful in a social setting such as communication, fashion, or physical fitness." That sounds about right, but it's wrong.

If an art critic arrives at your get-together in khakis and an undershirt, helps himself to six fingers of Jameson, tries to flirt with your teenage daughter, and then urinates with the bathroom door open, he's behaving like a socially awkward intellectual and exhibiting a pronounced disengagement with fashion and physical fitness. But "nerdy" doesn't feel like the best description of his behavior. The graphic designer you've recently met, who visits your apartment for the first time and talks for three hours about the suicidal impulses she's weathered since she dropped out of grad school, then describes your Klimt poster as sort of "freshman year of collegey," is also a socially awkward intellectual. But she isn't acting like a nerd. The problem with the current Wikipedia entry, in other words, is that nerdiness isn't really a matter of intellectualism and social awkwardness.

I believe there are two main categories of nerds: one type, disproportionately male, is intellectual in ways that strike people as machinelike, and socially awkward in ways that strike people as machinelike. These nerds are people who remind others, sometimes pleasantly, of machines.

They tend to remind people of machines by:

1. Being passionate about some technically sophisticated activity that doesn't revolve around emotional confrontation, physical confrontation, sex, food, or beauty (most activities that excite passion in non-nerds—basketball, violin, sex, surfing, acting, knitting, interior decorating, wine tasting, etc.—are built around one of these subjects).

2. Speaking in language unusually similar to written Standard English.

3. Seeking to avoid physical and emotional confrontation.

4. Favoring logic and rational communication over nonverbal, nonrational forms of communication or thoughts that don't involve reason.

5. Working with, playing with, and enjoying machines more than most people do.

Do I mean that nerds in this category are robots made of flesh and blood? No.

Brian Wilson is not into the ocean. "I'm afraid of the water," he says when people ask him about surfing. One interviewer has described his "Rain Man–like personality" as being reminiscent of a "voice-mail menu." Wilson is from Hawthorne, California, ten minutes from the Pacific, which makes his hydrophobia impressive. But his mother, Audree, has long maintained that he hummed the entire melody of "The Marines' Hymn" before he could talk, and that his mastery of musical instruments proceeded apace. When his younger brother Dennis persuaded him to write a song about a new teen pastime, he came up with "Surfin'," which became the Wilson brothers' first hit and led to their reinvention as the Beach Boys. Wilson proceeded to paint a fantasia in song, an amber-encased America ruled by athletes with multiple vehicles and multiple girlfriends. In the mid-1960s, as the rest of the Beach Boys toured Asia, he surrounded himself with studio musicians and recorded *Pet Sounds,* making Coke bottles into percussion instruments, recording in a pit of sand to get the right sound, writing string charts, and letting other people write his lyrics. The more the world fell for his make-believe, the more time he spent alone in his studio, sequestered from the world, living with equipment.

Wilson did things a machine cannot do. His work was more intuitive than logical. Nerds of this kind, crucially, are not actually like machines; they just remind people of them. They get stuck with the name "nerd" because their outward behavior can make them seem less than, and more than, human.

The second type of nerd probably consists equally of males and females. This is a nerd who is a nerd by sheer force of social exclusion.

In 1959, a twelve-year-old ninth grader named Anne Beatts

moved from a small, cozy private school in Dutchess County, New York, to a public high school in Somers, then one of the more remote New York City commuter towns.

"That was when I first heard the expression 'nerd,'" says Beatts. "The joke definition of *nerd* was someone who farts in the bathtub and bursts the bubbles. But really it was a person considered by the popular kids to be uncool. A lot of things would make you a nerd, and they were basically being thought of as someone who worked, who did homework in study hall. Teenage acne was a qualification, appearance. I was wearing undershirts and everyone else was wearing training bras, at least."

Friendless, she tried to get her homework done at school instead of at home, so she would work during homeroom and lunch. The only other person who opted for that isolation was "a mathematical genius who muttered to himself." His name was Marshall.

"So somebody noticed this and they said, 'Do you like Marshall?' And I didn't know high-school vocabulary, and I didn't know the loadedness of the word *like*. I didn't want to go, 'No, I don't like him,' or 'I dislike him,' so I said, 'Sure.' And they went, 'Oh, she likes him. There goes Marshall's girlfriend.' And so this became an epithet and a cry of humiliation to me in my first year of high school, Marshall's Girlfriend. And so I'd been labeled as a nerd."

By the time grade-skipping had made her a fifteen-year-old senior in 1962, Beatts had become editor of the high-school newspaper, and by pursuing every activity that might engender acceptance, up to and including cooking hot dogs for the football game, she had attained a perch where she was no longer mocked as a matter of routine. She chose this time to publish an editorial in the paper called "Leave the Nerds Alone," which caused her to be suspended from her editorship for its controversial subject matter.

In the early 1970s she wrote for *National Lampoon,* and she landed at *Saturday Night Live* in 1975. There, she created the "Nerds" sketches with her sometimes writing partner Rosie Shuster, helping to bring the word *nerd* into mainstream usage, which will be discussed more thoroughly later. "Marshall Blechtman" became a character on the sitcom about nerds Beatts created, *Square Pegs*.

Anne Beatts is an example of the second kind of nerd. Beatts became a nerd not because she was like Marshall but because she got shoved into the same category as Marshall (a type-one nerd) by peers who were looking for somebody to exclude.

The heroes of American popular culture are surfers, cowboys, pioneers, gangsters, cheerleaders, and baseball players, people at home in the heat of physical exertion. But so many of the individuals who make these images are more like Anne Beatts. Their voyeurism—their sense of staring from the wrong lunch table at a radiant nation—makes for a vision of America that appeals to the whole world, including America itself. There's a globe full of outsiders thirsty for glimpses of the land of myth, and American nerds have gratified them with adoring images. Wilson—the bodiless studio addict who spent days refining drum sounds for songs about high-school football and girls on the beach—was the rule, not the exception, for North American fabulists, for DreamWorks as much as Microsoft. In this book, I'll try to catalog the way a largely nerdy chain of media figures has affected the way we think about nerds.

I'll also address the relationship between nerdiness and ethnicity. You don't need to belong to any particular class or ethnicity to be a nerd, but some ethnic stereotypes are nerdier than others. In the late nineteenth century, educators strove to nourish the "primitive" in white middle-class boys and thus mold them into athletic men of character, the opposite of the "greasy grinds" who studied their way out of the Lower East Side. In the 1980s, opinion columnists warned that the Japanese were taking over the world through their unrivaled love of machines and their mechanistically corporate cast of mind. If a propaganda artist of the Third Reich had time-traveled to 1984 and watched *Revenge of the Nerds,* he might have interpreted the hero, Louis Skolnick, as a traditional age-old caricature of a Jew, and Ogre and his band of overwhelmingly blond-haired and blue-eyed jocks as the image of ideal Aryans (in appearance, if not conduct), even though the film never explicitly raises the question of ancestry or religion. The linguist Mary Bucholtz has observed that some contemporary high-school students who consider themselves nerds cleave so tightly to American Standard English, even as the popular white kids cultivate hip-hop affectations, that they engage in what she called "hyperwhiteness"—whiteness so white it destroys the aura of normality that usually attends white people. The history of the concept of nerdiness helps show some of the ways we have thought about the primitive, the "Oriental," white people, Jews, nature, and the machine.

"We" here does not mean "Americans." Rosie Shuster, Lorne Michaels, and Elvis Costello—two Canadians and an Englishman—all made their mark on the history of the nerd at the same pivotal moment. Tokyo is the city where *otaku,* a type similar to the American nerd, has its own neighborhood, Akihabara, known for waitresses who dress as manga characters.[1] In England, the word

---

1. One such restaurant described in *The New York Times* had them address customers as "master."

*boffin* has been around for centuries. Theories about the fine differences in meaning between *geek, dork,* and *nerd* in Silicon Valley and other tech hives are all over the Internet, but, internationally, the nerd/otaku/geek/dork is a concept that involves: loneliness; the rote, mechanical nature of work in the industrial and postindustrial ages; the way modernity allows the body to fall into disuse; and the way contemporary mass media invite people into voyeuristic relationships with simple fictions and numb them to the pleasures of real life. To understand nerds is to enrich our understanding of many demons.

Beyond the traits that fit into an intellectually defensible definition of *nerd,* there's a nerd tone, a nerd aesthetic. You know it when you see it: the indestructible-looking but nonetheless largely destroyed glasses, the pair of pleated shorts that exposes thigh, the childlike laugh, the intense self-seriousness. These are the universally acknowledged symptoms, and it's worth tracing how they come together in a chain of pop-culture images.

What is the history of the nerd? What are the different nerd subcultures like, and what are the rules and rituals that hold together the communities within those subcultures? What do the stories of two of my friends from childhood have to do with all this?

I will take a serious approach to a subject usually treated lightly, which is a nerdy thing to do.

# the mark of greatness

On a soccer field beside a nature preserve, a dozen boys stand in a circle holding lengths of piping converted into blunt weapons. A brisk wind sings through the dying leaves; these are the last days of fall in Amherst, Massachusetts, and the chill puts us in an Arthurian cast of mind. There are few smiles in our ring of scrofulous faces. We know this is not serious, but for some reason we are serious.

Our weapons are called boff swords, our purpose here boffing. To craft the instruments in our hands, we've purchased PVC pipe from Aubuchon Hardware at the despondent mall off Route 9, encased the ivory plastic tube with soft pipe insulation, and sealed together the bludgeon with duct tape. We're about to fight a melee, last-man-standing. Get hit in the arm, you lose the use of that arm. Lose one leg, you hop. Lose both, and you are on your knees. A hit to the skull or torso, and you fall dead. For a moment, there is no sound but the inconsolable wind. Then Jon L., with his freckles and his orange vest, looks at each of us and speaks calmly: "One, two, three."

Nobody is so naïve as to rush into the center. We all want to win. Some boys back up and walk sideways in order to stab somebody from behind. Some boys move with two hands on a long sword trembling four feet before them; some wave two shorter swords, some a sword and shield. We are thirteen, fourteen; it's possible for each of us to believe that, for all intents and purposes, this soccer field might as well be a glade set aside for the resolution of disputes among the aristocracy of the sword. If the sons of the Prince of Wales had fallen into a conflict over farmland in the thirteenth century, we reason, it would have looked like this, basically.

We also know it's a game, and the kind of game geeks would play, but we are proud of the fact that we are above labels. In fact, people often use labels for us, like "total fucking loser," and they bounce right off. Who are they to find us so contemptible? How long would they last in this contest of intense young men, this gauntlet of pipe and tape? In my heart, I believe life will eventually favor those of us in this field. We're the ones intent on making a game of combat, and the career world, I anticipate, will be a combat realm. Who cares about our detractors? We'll bury them.

Thinking about this sort of thing makes me excited, and like the rest of the boys, I start to swing and parry as the circle tightens and we begin to attack our neighbors. Jon falls upon me with his long sword. I swipe it away and spring back into an ingenious defensive posture, crouching low to the ground with my sword ready at a diagonal before me, so that my torso is out of reach and I can knock an opponent off balance when he goes on the attack, then spring forward for the kill.

"He's taking a shit! He's taking a shit!" says Jon, pointing at me. I know I shouldn't mind, and I pretend not to, but I rise up from the crouch and must have a vengeful look in my eyes because Jon begins to laugh hysterically, like a girl, stealing backward glances as he runs, and I chase him and cut him all to pieces, in the game.

As I turn over my memory of the incident, I remember a feeling of righteousness. Each boy in that ring knew what was expected of him: to fight, honorably, and to treat opponents as equals. Nobody was picked in order of preference; nobody was captain; nobody was on a team. You could speak in slang and joke around if you wanted to, but you could also speak like somebody out of *Ivanhoe*, formally, with politeness unfettered by irony. Nobody would make fun of you—not *really* make fun of you—if you spoke that way. We couldn't decide for ourselves if we wanted to play an elaborate game of make-believe or if we just wanted to swing swords, but we weren't going to deny one another the right to either choice. There were rules that came with boffing, and while we didn't talk about them, we knew what they were and we knew how to follow them. This was not the case with the rules that governed life beyond the circle we'd drawn in the field.

Everybody knows that boffers, like nerds who play fantasy role-playing games like Dungeons & Dragons and attach latex points to their ears to make themselves more elflike, are engaged in a game of pretend, a chance to inhabit another body. They're voyeurs. But sports nerds play online rotisserie baseball games in which they're managers of real teams. High-school debaters do the same thing, only they're role-playing cabinet secretaries. Even music nerds, who sometimes pretend to be cool, seem to hope that a familiarity with defunct record labels and one-hit wonders creates kinship between musicians and themselves.

In all these cases, the beloved activity is one that involves little or no physical or emotional confrontation—whether it's collecting singles from the 1980s, pretending to be a medieval warlord, developing software, or delving into the statistical patterns of the 1937 World Series. It's socially inclusive and embraces logical frameworks, structuring play with points, hierarchies, and categories. And if you are a deeply nerdy person, your nerdy activity dictates who your friends are and are not, so that it becomes evident from just being around you that you prefer abstract physics or policy debate or computer games to skateboarding or going to parties or playing soccer.

All these generalizations applied to my friends and me in ninth grade. More remarkable, we all fit the look people usually associate with nerds. We were a slow-drifting cloud of glasses, high pants, and trench coats. We liked that we had a look. I used to call us the "Darknerds," because I actually thought we were menacing, which, this being pre-Columbine, was funny to people who overheard me. I often wondered whether there had been people like us in other centuries. The answer is yes.

# newt envy, and were there nerds in the nineteenth century?

How did we get these rule-loving, unathletic men and women? How long has the type been around?

There are nerds in literature going back at least two hundred years. Mary Bennet, in *Pride and Prejudice,* published in 1813, is a good example. She's one of the younger sisters of Elizabeth, the main character. Her nerdiness first becomes evident in Chapter 5:

> "Pride," observed Mary, who piqued herself upon the solidity of her reflections, "is a very common failing I believe. By all that I have ever read, I am convinced that it is very common indeed, that human nature is particularly prone to it, and that there are very few of us who do not cherish a feeling of self-complacency on the score of some quality or other, real or imaginary."

It's not just pedantry that makes Mary a nerd; it's a lack of gracefulness that her conspicuously logical ways of thinking can't correct. At a ball in Chapter 6, Elizabeth plays the piano, to heartfelt applause:

> She was eagerly succeeded at the instrument by her sister Mary, who having, in consequence of being the only plain one in the family, worked hard for knowledge and accomplishments, was always impatient for display . . . though vanity had given her application, it had given her likewise a pedantic air and conceited manner . . . Elizabeth, easy and unaffected, had been listened to with much more pleasure, though not playing half so well . . .

Mary is comfortable with the technical but not the intuitive. She likes to use the language of scientific detachment and to draw on generalities she's picked up in books. She's hard to marry off. In modern adaptations of *Pride and Prejudice,* such as the 1940 film by Robert Z. Leonard, she's sometimes given glasses.

Austen uses her nerd for comic relief. In the pack of middle- and upper-class families the Bennet sisters live in, the actual purpose of a conversation between a young man and a young woman is usually tangential, if related, to the ostensible point of that conversation. The local news and gossip are MacGuffins; the point is mutual testing and mild sensual exploration. Inanities are necessary for the look or witticism that will ultimately lead to lifelong marriage and financial security or insecurity. Unlike the other Bennet sisters, who are alive to the unwritten rule that the purportedly rational conversations between unwed young people in this town usually have nothing to do with what they appear to be about, Mary tries to get down to brass tacks and help everybody reason through the dilemma at hand. Nobody is really looking for the solution to whatever problem might be under discussion at a dance at the Meryton assembly, ever. Contact, not deliberation, is the goal.[1] Mary might grasp this if somebody would only spell it out for her, but nobody does.

"Little need be premised about Tibby," states the narrator of E. M. Forster's *Howards End*. "He was now an intelligent man of sixteen, but dyspeptic and difficile." If this were really all there was to say about Tibby's condition, he might not be a nerd, but the way Tibby is "difficile" (meaning "difficult") happens to be nerdy.

*Howards End,* published in 1910, concerns two English families, one of which, the Schlegels, consists mainly of three grown siblings: two girls, Margaret and Helen, and one boy, Tibby. During a famous scene wherein Tibby, Helen, and Margaret attend a performance of Beethoven's Fifth Symphony, Tibby is fixated on the mechanics of the composition, the counterpoint; he keeps the score open on his knee, and afterward asks, "Surely you haven't forgotten the drum steadily beating on the low C?" Meanwhile, Tibby's sister Helen is awash in images of shipwrecks and goblins. This is the same dynamic that will play out ninety years later in freshman dorm rooms all over the world, where one roommate will harp on Elvin Jones's use of the toms in Coltrane's *A Love*

1. See William Deresiewicz's essay "Community and Cognition in *Pride and Prejudice*" (*ELH* 64, Summer 1997). He writes, "The first parts of their bodies to touch are their voices."

*Supreme,* or Sonic Youth's innovations with feedback, while the other roommate looks out the window and talks about how *Daydream Nation* is like golden foxes running down a freeway, or sweet to make out to.

Tibby is like Mary Bennet in his tendency to speak clearly, non-allusively, and untactfully. When Helen upbraids Tibby for not being more hospitable to another young man, "Tibby sighed, and drew a long strand of hair over his forehead. 'Oh, it's no good looking superior. I mean what I say.'"

Meaning what you say, and wanting other people to mean what they say, to stop alluding, implying, and teasing, and get down to the point—Tibby and Mary and nerds in general rally under this banner. Another fictional proponent of the mean-what-you-say philosophy, and one of the clearest examples of a nerd in prewar English literature, is Gussie Fink-Nottle, a creation of P. G. Wodehouse.

Augustus Fink-Nottle first appears in *Right Ho, Jeeves,* published in 1934. As Bertie Wooster explains to Jeeves, Gussie's preoccupation with newts began when he and Bertie were at school:

> He kept them in a study in a kind of glass-tank arrangement, and pretty niffy the whole thing was, I recall. I suppose one ought to have been able to see what the end would be even then . . . The craving grew upon him. The newts got him. Arrived at man's estate, he retired to the depths of the country and gave his life up to these dumb chums. I suppose he used to tell himself that he could take them or leave them alone, and then found—too late—that he couldn't.

Apart from wearing glasses, Gussie also happens to look like "something on a slab." He suffers from a phobia of emotional confrontation. Half of the events in *Right Ho, Jeeves* hang on Gussie's attempts to win the hand of Madeline Bassett, a girl who is suspected of writing poetry and who comments at one point that the stars are "God's daisy chain." When by good fortune Gussie is able to eavesdrop on a conversation between Madeline and Bertie in which Madeline confesses her affection for Gussie, he is supposed to come forward and propose. Instead, he talks about the sexual dimorphism of newts, and Madeline decides to go to bed. Bertie and Jeeves are left to contemplate how such a "cloth-headed guffin" might possibly be helped. ("With infinite toil," explains Bertie, "you maneuvered him into a position where all he had to do was charge ahead, and he didn't charge ahead but went off sideways, missing the objective completely.") In the end, they get him drunk.

What makes Gussie most profoundly nerdy is his desire for communication that doesn't depend on the emotional expression or allusiveness just about mandated by a daisy-chain-metaphor girl like Madeline Bassett. Considering with terror the prospect of asking Madeline to marry him, he says to Bertie, "Do you know how a male newt proposes, Bertie? He just stands in front of the female newt vibrating his tail and bending his body in a semi-circle. I could do that on my head. No, you wouldn't find me grousing if I were a male newt."

Wanting to be a male newt seems a markedly different dream from working with machines, but Gussie's understanding of being a newt revolves around rule-bound, programmatic—machinelike— communication. A newt, in Gussie's imagining of a newt's consciousness, knows exactly what commands to execute if he wants to proclaim his desire to mate. Among humans, a declaration of love demands statements that don't follow readily delineated conventions. Although living in a place and time without anything that resembles a modern computer, Gussie longs for a computer-like exchange.

Nobody expects delicate character studies from Wodehouse, but one of the things that's striking about Mary and Tibby is that Austen and Forster, authors usually so committed to empathy and psychological insight, created such uncomplicated humorous sidekicks, people about whom, in Forster's words, little need be premised. With the great newt speech, Wodehouse went much deeper. Wouldn't it be interesting to read a substantial premise on Tibby? To understand more of the circumstances that shaped him? What is it about Mary and Tibby that makes such fastidious students of human interaction as Austen and Forster feel okay about rendering their emotional lives in sketch? Neither Mary nor Tibby gets anywhere near the empathy nor the space on the page devoted to their siblings—even Kitty Bennet gets twice as many mentions as Mary.

The best explanation is the *romantic reaction* against nerds. The MIT professor Sherry Turkle came up with the term to describe the way society makes an arbitrary distinction between thinking and feeling and uses it to make people who are good at reasoning, like MIT students, appear as if they're not entitled to a normal emotional life. Austen and Forster tend to slightly dehumanize Mary and Tibby for the same reason people tend to think of software engineers as inadequate in their depth of feeling. To understand the pack of assumptions behind those tendencies, it helps to examine a book roughly contemporaneous with *Pride and Prejudice,* Mary Shelley's 1816 novel *Frankenstein*. In that story, immediately and enduringly popular, you find the seeds of the modern prejudice.

# the case against scientists in towers

The story, a classic of high-school literary history, goes that Mary Shelley wrote *Frankenstein* one summer at Lord Byron's house in the Alps shortly after the death of her first child. One night Byron had a conversation with Shelley's celebrity poet husband, Percy, about some recent experiments in which dead frogs and recently hanged men were made to twitch by running electricity through their bodies. Afterward, Mary had a recurring nightmare in which she massaged her dead baby back to life.

The book was a hit, and its fame was abetted by that of Percy and that of Mary's literary parents, the late Mary Wollstonecraft (author of *A Vindication of the Rights of Woman*) and William Godwin (a pioneer of anarchism). Mary Shelley, quiet girl among loud personalities, neglected by her remarried father, became the Mother of Frankenstein; the story was adapted for at least ten different theatrical productions during her lifetime.

The keynote of *Frankenstein* is a yearning for family, and the horror in the story (the plot is awkwardly stitched together, as it were, and gets by on its fantastic premise) derives from the tendency of the brainy antihero to cut himself off from his loving family's influence. It's the work of a teenager with a distant intellectual as her lone parent.

The young Victor Frankenstein describes his boyish passion for science as "a fervent longing to penetrate the secrets of nature," which makes his thirst for knowledge sound like a stand-in for a more urgent masculine need. ("Here were men who had penetrated deeper and knew more," he remarks, upon reading the modern scientists.) But unlike the pursuit of a lover, the pursuit of a scientific breakthrough slowly rots the body—"My cheek had grown pale with study, and my person had become emaciated with confinement." Attributes that might make a young man an appealing husband and father—looks, health—fall prey to the demands of science. Meanwhile, his loving, virtuous father, his best friend, and his adopted sister, all described in glowing prose, grow concerned and miss him. He doesn't care—his lab becomes all that's "real."

When the creature he has made from cadavers opens its eyes, Victor looks at his breathing creation and decides there may be some bugs yet to be worked out.

> His yellow skin scarcely covered the work of muscles and arteries beneath; his hair was of lustrous black, and flowing; his teeth of a pearly whiteness; but these luxuriances only formed a horrid contrast with his watery eyes, that seemed almost of the same colour as the dun-white sockets in which

they were set, his shriveled complexion and straight black lips.

Victor staggers out of the lab in terror. This irritating turnaround—first lock yourself in a tower and figure out how to make a living person out of dead flesh, bigger than sexually conceived humans because you found it easier to slap together bigger components, then be unable to deal with it when it looks at you, and run away—is Victor Frankenstein in a nutshell. It's what makes him an ur-nerd.

The young scientist's mistake betrays a combination of rational thinking and technical prowess coupled with a childlike inability to fully grasp that other people are just as needy, ambitious, and sensitive as himself—as Harold Bloom once put it, Frankenstein is "a being who has never achieved a full sense of another's existence." That's what enables him to make the monster and fail to think, *How would I like it if I had skin that barely held together, was eight feet tall, and had yellow eyes and black lips, so that people were inclined to run from me in terror? How would I like it if I had no family?* His failure is a failure to emotionally confront another person, a failure of empathy. In a stupid person, this lack of empathy might not matter, but in a modern man with a godlike capacity for making things, it can create disasters. The root of evil in *Frankenstein* is the mingling of scientific brilliance with a deficit of emotional connectedness.

Shelley's critique of Victor still hangs in the air. There is a perceptible chain of influential thinkers and educators that leads from English Romanticism to the American concept of the nerd. Tibby in

*Howards End* comes at the end of or after the Romantic era, but he's the descendent of Victor Frankenstein in his disengagement with the sensual and familial in favor of the academic. As for Gussie, the newt world is the monstrosity that makes him go pale in the cheek. To understand how close the contemporary concept of the nerd is to Dr. Frankenstein, you have only to watch the first forty-five minutes of John Hughes's 1985 comedy *Weird Science*.

Watching *Frankenstein* on TV, two virginal high-school nerds decide to use a home computer to create a woman. Lisa, the product of their experiment, played by Kelly LeBrock, shares with Frankenstein's creature an awareness of the sensual realm superior to that of her inventor(s). After the three of them get into the shower together and the boys can't take off their clothes, she decides to bring them to a bar where there are a lot of black people. Soon a combination of bourbon and cultural immersion begins to coax forth the Soul within the dork. A smash cut goes to Anthony Michael Hall wearing a pimp suit and chewing on a cigar, deftly playing upon the sympathies of the black guys. "Yo, man, she kneed me in the nuts," he explains, talking about a girl who rejected him, and the black people commune with him in his suffering. In order to become an emotionally vulnerable, emotionally connected person, able to take his clothes off in front of a woman, he has to swing to the polar opposite of a nerd: a black dude. In the logic of the film, getting dunked in blackness brings the machine-man in contact with the earthy, the animal.

Mary Shelley and like-minded romantics lobbied for soulfulness, for the kind of emotional life—empathy, communion with family and nature—that Victor Frankenstein threw over for his lab. (Of course, it's not quite right to draw a dichotomy between nerds and romantics; Anne Beatts described her *Saturday Night Live* creation Lisa Loopner as "a romantic," and nerds who are nerds by dint of social exclusion don't have to have Frankenstein tendencies at all.) But there's a kind of antinerd who stands in contrast to both Mary Shelley and Victor Frankenstein: a person whose personality has been molded by his excellence at sports. How did the jock come to stalk the earth?

# the rise of phys ed

"I'm not sure I like boys who think too much."
—Endicott Peabody,
founder and headmaster, the Groton School

In 1892, Ohio public schools established the first physical education requirements, followed by the public schools of Illinois in 1895 and of North Dakota in 1899. The first tennis court was built in Boston in 1876, the first basketball court in Springfield, Massachusetts, in 1891. Shortly before World War I, the head of the City of Philadelphia's Department of Moral Education, Charles K. Taylor, conducted an "experiment in character building" in which schoolboys were made to wear buttons that noted whether they had first-class, second-class, or third-class physiques. Teddy Roosevelt, author of *The Strenuous Life,* along with various eugenicist experts, cited phys ed as a "racial defense weapon" against the weakening of the Nordics.[1] These were catastrophic developments for nerds. What was with the turn of the century and its preoccupation with health and manliness? To work out how America developed its concept of a nerd, it helps to establish how America arrived at its concept of a sportsman.

Late nineteenth-century America was plagued by a fear of human domestication, of men becoming overcivilized and house-bound. Agrarian life slowly gave out; 80 percent of the country's males were farmers in 1800, but agriculture employed only half the labor force in 1880. In 1830, one out of fifteen Americans lived in a town of eight thousand or more. In 1910, half of America did. The frontier, an escape hatch for men who wanted to leave behind the comforts and restraints of civilization in the East, vanished parcel by parcel. Maybe most important in the history of the jock and the nerd, the crafts that provided a living for artisans operating small businesses gave way to low-skilled industrial labor in impersonal factories and clerical jobs in bureaucracies that ran on obedience and rote desk work. For men who felt emasculated by the industrial age, sport was a way of making tough-guy skills important again. Boxing heroes like John L. Sullivan used their bodies in displays of skill and aggression; their profession was the opposite of repetitive, subservient industrial wage-earning. Sports represented an arena where a few blue-collar men could make a living through cunning and physical prowess. To admire John L. Sullivan was to admire a draft horse who didn't answer to the managerial class. To watch a baseball game, in a field or a park, was to escape into a wide-open, pseudonatural green space—a swatch of West-

1. Clifford Putney, *Muscular Christianity: Manhood and Sports in Protestant America, 1880–1920.*

ern prairie in the middle of the city. Biceps and reflexes didn't help much in the workplace anymore, but even if you couldn't make biceps and reflexes *needed,* you could still make them desirable, envied, beloved.

"Nobody can grow to a perfectly normal manhood today without the benefits of at least a small amount of baseball experience and practice," stated *Training the Boy,* a 1913 advice manual. President Taft lauded its healthful effects in 1912 and declared himself a fan. "All boys love baseball," the novelist Zane Grey wrote in a baseball magazine in 1909. "If they don't, they're not real boys."

If, for American workers, sports represented a way to reclaim physical mastery from the increasingly industrial, urban, and bureaucratized civilization that had started to push highly skilled physical work to the margins, it represented something just as important for the upper class at the turn of the century: a way to prepare young gentlemen to be leaders and a way for the upper class to define itself against the immigrants crammed together in the cities. If *Entertainment Weekly* had done a story called "The Protestant Establishment from 1870 to 1920: Looking Back on Fifty Years of Budding Imperial Ambition and Anglophilia," there would have been a sidebar that read: "Out—Effeminacy, Jews, the library, immigrant hordes; In—Football, England, nature, island colonies, Native Americans." Influential members of said establishment were increasingly willing to overlook the War of 1812 and the burning of Washington. They were attracted to England, which had an expanding empire and was reaching the peak of its influence in world affairs, and the part of English culture they embraced most fervently was a recent invention called Muscular Christianity.

The cutest mascot for Muscular Christianity was the nineteenth-century Harry Potter: Tom Brown. *Tom Brown's School Days,* written by the English lawyer Thomas Hughes, was a young-adult novel Teddy Roosevelt prescribed for every American schoolboy. The book didn't really need his endorsement: it went into a fifth printing in the first year of its publication and never went out of print. Muscular Christianity and the progressive-era educational philosophies it influenced combined with Romanticism to help create the nerd by asserting that the soul of an ideal youth should house a lust for physical confrontation. This was not to say a solid boy would languish in primitivism like a Hottentot his whole life; but physical contests were a necessary phase, or component, in the natural flowering of an Anglo-Saxon man.

Tom Brown is a nice jock. Descended from an aristocratic but scrappy family based in the Vale of White Horse, a place of many hearty folk, Tom becomes an alpha boy at the Rugby School by fighting hard on the playing field and by helping to contain Flashman, the school bully. Rugby eventually expels Flashman for drinking, but before his career is cut short, he habitually punches and insults boys smaller than himself. The most revelatory day in Tom's education, which rarely to never takes place in a classroom, is the day he conspires with another young boy to square accounts with Flashman. It's boys like Tom who'll grow up to be the kind of men who will fight for England's empire, acquiring through sport what was then called manliness and character and what is now called team spirit, school spirit, or teen spirit. Team/teen/school spirit is helpful if you want to put down an insurrection in China, and Hughes is quite clear that this is why Tom Brown is precious to England:

> Wherever the fleets and armies of England have
> won renown, there stalwart sons of the Browns have

done yeoman's work. With the yew bow and cloth-yard shaft at Cressy and Agincourt—with the brown bill and pike under the brave Lord Willoughby—with culverin and demi-culverin against Spaniards and Dutchmen—with hand-grenade and sabre, and musket and bayonet, under Rodney and St. Vincent, Wolfe and Moore, Nelson and Wellington, they have carried their lives in their hands; getting hard knocks and hard work in plenty, which was on the whole what they looked for, and the best thing for them; and little praise or pudding, which indeed they, and most of us, are better without.

(Hughes didn't fight his impulse to lionize Tom, and he didn't buy any modern literary theory about characters being flesh and blood rather than the embodiment of ideals: "Why my whole object in writing at all was to get the chance of preaching!" he wrote. "When a man comes to my time of life and has his bread to make, and very little time to spare, is it likely that he will spend almost the whole of his yearly vacation in writing a story just to amuse people? I think not.")

There is a nerd in *Tom Brown's School Days*, a boy named Martin who keeps a machine of his own making in his room. According to Hughes, he's "one of those unfortunates who were at that time of day (and are, I fear, still) quite out of their places at a public school [like Rugby]." In another environment, Hughes theorizes, "Martin would have been seized upon and educated as a natural philosopher."

He was also an experimental chemist on a small scale, and had made unto himself an electric machine, from which it was his greatest pleasure and glory to administer small shocks to any small boys who were rash enough to venture into his study . . . Of course, poor Martin, in consequence of his pursuits, had become an Ishmaelite in the house.

Note that his "pleasure and glory" derive from his machine. Other boys use Martin's tendency to keep animals in his room as a premise for playing practical jokes on him, but Tom introduces him to another intellectual boy, Arthur, so that each may have a friend.

"Well, I say," sputtered out Martin eagerly, "will you come to-morrow, both of you, to Caldecott's Spinney, then, for, I know of a kestrel's nest . . ."

Hughes likes Martin; the bullies, Flashman and "Slugger" Williams, are the only really bad boys in *Tom Brown's School Days*. In fact, Martin and Arthur serve as an excellent reason for Tom to learn how to stand up to bullies on behalf of others, because they are so often in need of protection. They're just not as high on the pyramid of heroism as Tom; it's Tom who is the standard building block for Britain's ruling class, the kind of lad you need in large numbers to maintain the empire on which the sun never sets.

Hughes never wholeheartedly embraced the term *Muscular Christianity*, first used in 1857, but it stuck as the name for any doctrine that celebrated pious gentlemen who learned the manly art of rugby football as boys to become an unstoppable offense for the empire, which was understood to be a device of Jesus. Hughes hated the idea that Christian piety demanded young men be sheep grazing on ecumenical literature, that a good Christian was a bookish, indoorsy minister. This was an era in which evangelicals were so ambivalent about the morality of sports that they considered them, as George Eliot wrote, "a plague infection"; it's hard to imagine our current image of an ideal popular boy without Hughes staging his rebellion first.

After Tom Brown and Teddy Roosevelt, the most valuable pitchman for Muscular Christianity in the United States was Endicott Peabody. An American educated at Rugby under the regime of Thomas Arnold, the same headmaster who inspired worship in Thomas Hughes, Peabody set out to forge, in Groton, Massachusetts, a private school for the sons of the American elite that would produce real men. Every boy at Groton was required to play football.

The school hit big. With America winning the 1898 Spanish-American War and coming into its own as an economic power at the same time it was being overrun by immigrants, there were rich American WASPs eager to make their male children more English both as a way to ape England's Risk-worthy triumph over portions of the world and to differentiate themselves from the Jews, Chinese, and other aliens who were becoming citizens of the republic in extraordinary numbers. Peabody was openly suspicious of intellectual boys, and the culture of Groton, highly influential among other elite American boarding schools, was designed to produce students who triumphed not through book smarts but through what F. Scott Fitzgerald would eventually call "animal magnetism."

Meanwhile, TR, maybe the most self-consciously masculine president ever, loved to cast foreign policy decisions and social distinctions in terms of real men and sissies (*sissy,* tellingly, was an affectionate term for one's sister in the first half of the nineteenth century and became an insult for another man toward the century's end). He lampooned those who would oppose American conquest abroad as "timid," "lazy," and "overcivilized." And he celebrated the progress of athleticism among privileged men. "Forty or fifty years ago the writer on American morals was sure to deplore the effeminacy and luxury of young Americans who were born to rich parents," he wrote. "The boy who was too well off then . . . felt shame in his inability to take part in rough pastimes and field sports. Nowadays, whatever other faults the son of rich parents may tend to develop, he is at least forced . . . to develop his body—and therefore, to a certain extent, his character—in the rough sports which call for pluck, endurance, and physical address." More famously, he pronounced, "We don't want to see the virtuous young man always have shoulders that slope like those of a champagne bottle, while the young man who is not virtuous is allowed to monopolize the burly strength which must be possessed by every great and masterful nation."

In colleges and boarding schools, there was a new name for students who declined to partake in student activities: *greasy grind,* or *greaser.* (*Grind* emerged in the late nineteenth century, and the *greasy* was fixed to it early in the twentieth.) In the early 1880s, Charles W. Eliot, the president of Harvard, reported to the board of trustees that under his leadership "the ideal student has been transformed from a stooping, weak, and sickly youth into one well-formed, robust, and healthy." In 1893, the series of dime-store novels about Frank Merriwell, a fictional Yale football star, sold 200,000 copies a week. Preachers would cut their sermons short the Sunday of the Yale-Princeton game in New York City, which filled a stadium with 40,000 people. The following decade saw the inauguration of Harvard Stadium, which seated 35,000, and in 1914 Yale opened the country's largest football stadium, which accommodated 70,000. A

Princeton survey of who was let in to exclusive societies at Harvard, Yale, and Princeton found that during the last years of the nineteenth century, the percentage of valedictorians who got into the societies plummeted at all three universities.[2]

These movements were protests against the inevitable. No landed gentry was going to win back its authority over technical experts. The Prussian general staff (that very same military organization credited with inventing the proto-D&D of *kriegspiel*) was composed of such men. They developed military strategies and military technology and were the central governing authority over the Prussian forces, and they were so effective that the rest of the European powers created their own counterparts.[3] War—the place where masculinity could be proven and defined—was increasingly a matter of strategy and technology, decreasingly a matter of valor. Building the courage to engage selflessly in the physical and emotional confrontations of combat was no longer as important as having the best thinkers, the most efficient bureaucratic structures, the most sophisticated weaponry. Things would never go back to the way they had been. So the nerd—the technical expert who shies from physical and emotional confrontation—was a concept fed by the resentment by people who preferred, at least aesthetically, the gentry to the techies.

The nerd was created partly by romantics like Mary Shelley— people suspicious of technical experts because they seemed cut off from family life, emotionally disengaged, perverted by a fun-

2. See Jerome Karabel, *The Chosen.*
3. See R. W. Connell, *The History of Masculinity.*

damentally male drive to penetrate the secrets of nature—and partly by Victorian preservationists of the knight, who hoped to create in the gentleman-athlete a male heir to the aristocracy of the sword. Nerds, almost by definition, came to power in the end, because modernity was on their side, but that didn't mean anybody had to like them. They could still be denied prestige and affection.

Such is the tragedy of the high-earning but self-loathing MIT grad. You win, moans some choir of disembodied voices from the realm of the Authentic and Natural and Desirable, but you are still a loser to us. Somewhere, on our decrepit estate among the gray rocks of Scotland or on a high-school football field in Indiana, we mock you.

## CRUDE GRAPHIC REPRESENTATION OF COMPLEX CHANGES

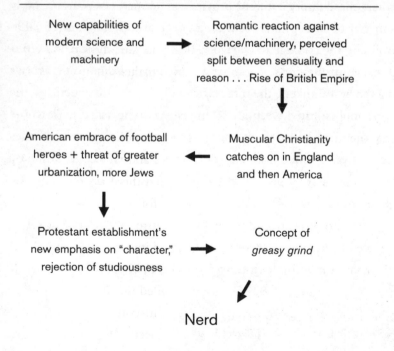

New capabilities of modern science and machinery ➡️ Romantic reaction against science/machinery, perceived split between sensuality and reason . . . Rise of British Empire

⬇️

American embrace of football heroes + threat of greater urbanization, more Jews ⬅️ Muscular Christianity catches on in England and then America

⬇️

Protestant establishment's new emphasis on "character," rejection of studiousness ➡️ Concept of *greasy grind*

↙️

Nerd

# dawn of the fan

The tide of opinion had turned against people who would now be thought of as nerds. A legal coup for people eager to preserve some semblance of the old rugged America, the Immigration Act of 1924 staunched the flow from Europe and Asia. But there was a silver lining: a guy from Luxembourg began to gather the unwanted into an invincible social web.

Hugo Gernsback came to New York City in 1904, at nineteen. In 1909 he founded the Wireless Association of America and *Modern Electronics,* the first known electronics and radio magazine. He imported radio parts from Europe and fed the popularity of amateur wireless, claiming 10,000 members for the association within its first year. In his magazine, he started to publish short stories under the label *scientifiction,* which evolved into *science fiction.* He did write a novel in this style, in 1911, called *Ralph 124C 41 +,* and the biggest award given to sci-fi writers is called the Hugo, but Gernsback was one of those men whose enthusiasm for his work expressed itself in raw mass. His archives occupy fifty linear feet of

Syracuse University Library; he published at least fifty periodicals, whose titles include *Scientific Detective Monthly, Sexologia, Sexology, Pirate Stories, Popular Medicine, French Humor, Gadgets, Know Yourself, Life Guide, Light, Luz, Milady, Motor Camper & Tourist, New Ideas for Technocracy Review, Woman's Digest, Your Body,* and *Your Dreams.* But Hugo Gernsback's monumental achievement was *Amazing Stories,* founded in 1926.

*Amazing Stories* started out publishing Jules Verne and H. G. Wells. When Gernsback found himself short on classic material, he started to accept submissions from aspiring writers. But the most influential prose he published was in Letters. Like the consistently painful and illuminating classifieds of *The New York Review of Books* today, the letters section of *Amazing Stories* was a place where readers could find evidence that there were people like themselves, only even stranger, more extreme, more desperate for companionship. And the *Amazing Stories* letters section came to function as a tiny Internet, supplying names and addresses to help people reach out to like-minded peers. Gernsback encouraged his subscribers to see themselves as engaged in an exchange of prophetic visions; "Extravagant Fiction Today," read the slogan on the masthead, "Cold Fact Tomorrow."

Sci-fi itself predates *Amazing Stories* by centuries. The earliest known story generally described as sci-fi is *Somnium*—the Dream— by the Renaissance astronomer Johannes Kepler. Published four years after his death in 1630, *Somnium* described a voyage to the moon that provided new perspectives on astronomy.[1] The Anglican bishop Francis Godwin wrote another moon travelogue, *The Man in*

---

1. See Arthur B. Evans, *The Origins of Science Fiction Criticism: From Kepler to Wells.*

*the Moone: A Discourse of a Voyage Thither,* published five years after his death in 1638. The same year saw the publication of John Wilkins's *Discovery of a New World in the Moone,* also contrived as a way of sharing ideas in an entertaining medium.

So, what was important about *Amazing Stories* was not that it contained sci-fi but that it induced people to write in and talk about obsessively collecting sci-fi. (One Harry Warner Jr., in his independently published sci-fi fandom history *All Our Yesterdays,* the more precise factual assertions of which I'd better hold at arm's length because it's not footnoted and looks like the laborious research of a smart but eccentric person, with microscopic font and subchapter headings like "Milwaulkee Fandom," documented the way constellations of fans began to seek one another out more rapidly than they'd been able to before.) In the June 1926 *Amazing Stories,* Hugo Gernsback wrote,

> There is not a day, now, that passes but we get from a dozen to fifty suggestions as to stories of which, frankly, we have no record . . . Some of these fans are constantly visiting the book stores with the express purpose of buying new or old scientifiction tales, and they even go to the trouble of advertising for some volumes that have long since gone out of print.

In the thirties and forties, these letter writers started to coalesce into local clubs and to hectograph and mimeograph *zines,* a word for amateur journalistic efforts that predates punk by half a century. One club, the Futurians, included Isaac Asimov as well as Frederik Pohl. Its members were all kids facing serious obstacles toward social acceptance: dental problems; immigrant accents; scrawny, uncomfortable-looking bodies. They passed in and out of the Communist Party, attending meetings sporadically, refining their own Marxist critiques of contemporary American life, imagining Utopian futures. Look at their photographs, and they're recognizable as a coterie of nerds.

The dedication of groups like the Futurians fueled Hugo Gernsback's mania for starting organizations, and he developed a correspondence club called the Science Fiction League—a kind of souped-up *Amazing Stories* letters section. Even this was not enough. Pohl set up an organization to bring the Science Fiction Leaguers face-to-face in local meetings; he started with a Brooklyn chapter and went on to found chapters in Philadelphia, Los Angeles, and Chicago. One day the New York chapter got on a train and went to Philly.

According to Pohl's memoirs, this "first SF con" took place in 1936 and lasted two hours.

> All that happened was that half a dozen of us fans from New York City got on the train to Philadelphia one Sunday afternoon. We were met at the station by half a dozen Philly fans. We repaired to a room, where we sat and talked for a while. (What we talked about is lost to history. Minutes were taken, but the secretary lost the minutes—I know this, because I was that secretary.) Then we got back on the train and went home, and that was it.

But the consequences, as Pohl put it, "were remarkable." What started in Philadelphia is now Comic-Con International in San Diego—where film executives troll for stories to option and search for the pulse of the action/horror audience—and all the less famous cons: AlCon, for Weird Al Yankovic fans; X-Files Con; Battlestar Galactica Con; and so on.

Pohl later argued that the reason sci-fi fans, and not, say, poetry fans, started cons is that science fiction is about trading ideas. True, but what's the exchange of ideas at AlCon? Cons are about warmth. You go to a con to enter an alternate universe where status is expertise on a book or a movie or a TV show, where the nerd habits of collecting and cataloging and rating are normal and esteemed.

Sci-fi fandom shared some roots with amateur radio (*Modern Electronics* was a radio magazine), but the ham radio world grew up parallel to it, retaining its distinct nerd subculture. Ham radio fans tended to champion their hobby as a refuge for rational, masculine communication in a wilderness of feminine, irrational, inefficient blabbing, and lionized the mastery of building and operating the technology involved.[2] Twentieth-century amateur radio operators—the hobby started in the teens but actually grew in popularity into the 1980s—remained in love with Morse code long after it outlived any obvious usefulness, arguing that dots and dashes, transmitted with pulses and transcribed into letters, were more accurate than spoken words. As Kristen Haring puts it in her history of the subculture, "Preference for code over spoken communication reflected a desire to rationalize language." Morse code scrapped the exchange of voices, the part of communication so

2. Kristen Haring, *Ham Radio's Technical Culture*, among other things an account of how the hobby was deliberately masculinized in PR efforts.

central to flirtation. Haring cites a letter originally published in the amateur-radio magazine *Contact Quarterly* (*CQ*) by one Carol Witte, a woman who excoriated her own sex, specifically "unlicensed wimmin (wives, gal friends, etc.)" for "cluttering up the phone bans with chin music."

Morse code funneled human communication through a machine, supposedly giving it uniformity and clarity. It wasn't just sticklers for actual Morse code who thought these were valuable qualities; there was a general sense among ham-radio hobbyists that they should create their own highly regimented language in order to create some semblance of Morse code's virtues, a machine language taught to humans, the ambiguity and regional flavors of vocal discourse replaced with something more rule-bound. Usually, that meant shorthand originally designed for telegraphs (QTH = "what's your location?").[3]

Of course, this affectation of rationality started to break down as soon as the old analog equipment used for ham radios fell to integrated circuits. Ham-radio lovers found themselves nostalgic for the "soul" and "warmth" of the old tubes that ham radios used to require,[4] not unlike indie rock musicians who reject sturdier solid-state amps and digital synths for tube amps and analog keyboards, which require frequent and expensive repairs (replacing and adjusting the tines on a thirty-year-old Rhodes organ is a daily-to-weekly ritual for a keyboardist). Ham radio was never quite so grimly utilitarian an undertaking as its followers wanted it to be.

But making language into a well-defined code is a pillar of nerdiness. Computer programming languages, and math, of course,

3. Haring, *Ham Radio's Technical Culture.*
4. Ibid.

are strictly rule-bound languages. Mary Bennet, Tibby, and Gussie Fink-Nottle would all have an easier time in this life if the human being had a clear, rational mating dance, like the lucky newt.

The newt impulse exists among sci-fi fans, but in a much subtler way. Reading and writing literature of any kind is not a rationally justifiable activity, but the way sci-fi/fantasy fans talk about the books they read suggests an unusually pragmatic, computer-like model for appreciating novels.

I attend a Thursday meeting of the Los Angeles Science Fantasy Society (LASFS), a sci-fi fan club in North Hollywood. One middle-aged man, sneaking in late, sits next to another in the row behind me and asks, "Do you mind if I sit next to you, good sir?" Twenty minutes later the two have the following conversation:

> Guy 1: *What are you reading these days?*
> Guy 2: *This series that's basically the Napoleonic wars with dragons.*
> Guy 1: *Oh, really? How is that?*
> Guy 2: *It's pretty good. It's basically one set of dragons as the French and the other as the English, and it's mostly dragon-on-dragon combat not dragon-on-man.*
> Guy 1: *Do they use magic?*
> Guy 2: *No, it's not so much spells as physical abilities. It's good.*

At another LASFS meeting, during the reviews section, when members stand and volunteer opinions on books, films, and TV shows, a mid-thirty-something with glasses and a beard describes what he's been reading this way: "The construction of this universe is interesting because the wizards have no powers of their own and can only summon djinns."

The focus here is on the mechanics of the situation. A large part of the fun of reading a sci-fi series is about inputting a particular set of variables (dragon-on-dragon without magic) into a model (the Napoleonic wars) and seeing what output you get.[5]

The creators of Dungeons & Dragons understood this form of fun and capitalized on it. They knew that the core of the role-playing game would be pitting one set of variables against another in a heavily structured mathematical arena and seeing what happened. The aesthetic components of D&D—elves, wizards, dwarves, epic journeys across hostile enchanted landscapes—look a lot like those of J. R. R. Tolkien's *Lord of the Rings* series. But its inventors, Dave Arneson and Gary Gygax, were cool on Tolkien: "His books always struck me as very droll and very boring," Gygax has said. Tolkien, an Oxford professor, often breezed through combat; the siege of Helm's Deep, which consumed a half hour and no doubt a thick slice of the effects budget in Peter Jackson's film adaptation, consumed barely three pages in Tolkien's thousand-page trilogy of books. Gygax preferred the bloodier work of fantasy-genre writers, and he perceived that the focus in most D&D adventures would be on fireballs and swordplay. While the game is open-ended and can't be won or lost, and allows players to act out any scenario they want—one could theoretically have a D&D adventure that consisted entirely of a love triangle between two of the players' characters and a shared object of desire played by the Dungeon Master—Gygax correctly predicted that it would generally be played in such a way that it would feed what he called "male

5. See Sherry Turkle, *The Second Self.*

competitiveness." D&D is a safe place for self-conscious teenagers to face up to their fantasies and anxieties in a group. But in practice, D&D tends to focus on the emotionally crudest, least realistic part of the game: combat. It affirms a fundamentally innocent view of the world. Life in D&D is usually a series of fights on the way to a clearly defined goal, not unlike video games such as Super Mario Bros. in which a character kicks, shoots, and jumps his way through a series of obstacles to an award that always lies somewhere to the right, attainable if only he can bushwack in the right direction.

Certainly in my own experience, sci-fi, D&D, and computers provided fun, brotherhood, and escape but didn't do much to hasten the crawl toward adulthood. There is a dilemma here that must have confused and pissed off my parents. You've got an eighth grader who doesn't like sports and who gets called a faggot by the kids who do. He never gets any exercise, and he's twitching most of the time. Eye contact; a firm handshake; combed, conditioned hair—these are glimmering points on the horizon. Picturing him with a girlfriend is like picturing him rowing the Charles. But this eighth grader does have friends. They draw monsters in the corners of spiral notebooks and scratch vampires into the canvas backing of three-ring binders with pens softened by their teeth. Their glasses are chrome and semirectangular, like orthodontic devices. At your son's thirteenth birthday, they all sing the dun-dun-dun from *2001: A Space Odyssey* when you bring in the cake, and they cheer and thump him on the back when he blows out the candles. They crack up when he tells the joke about the farmer's daughter and the watermelons. What do you do? Do you tell him to ditch his friends because as long as he's one of them, he may not kiss a girl for a very long time? Or do you tell him to stick with them? Do you let him figure it out on his own even though you feel pretty certain he understands neither the nature of the dilemma nor what is at stake?

As it happened, self-loathing offered a resolution. I would eventually put as much distance between myself and the inhabitants of that birthday tableau as my high school would afford. Movies don't generally show nerds as self-loathing, but they often are, and the MIT anthropologist Sherry Turkle offers one of the best explanations why.

# sherry turkle, t. s. eliot,
# and the split between feeling and thinking

Sherry Turkle's book *The Second Self* offers classic insights into the nerd condition, although Turkle, who drew on interviews with both established computer programmers and D&D-obsessed adolescents, almost never went so far as to use the word *nerd*. In a chapter on hacker culture, Turkle surveyed MIT undergrads who studied computer science, and she found an abundance of self-loathing. She concluded that this feeling was a symptom of a modern social illness.

Our society accepts a severed connection between science and sensuality. By extension, it accepts a divide between people who are good at dealing with things and people who are good at dealing with people.

This split in our culture has many social costs, of

which the first and most poignant is paid by children, particularly the suffering of many gifted adolescents.

The idea that afflicts the gifted children and MIT students whom Turkle examined is the Romantic reaction against the perceived Victor Frankensteins of the world, the Tibbys, Gussies, and Mary Bennets. Shelley's image of the scientist as sealed off in his lab, deaf to the pleasures of human contact, pursuing a grandiose but morally ill-conceived end, bears a notable resemblance to the self-image Turkle found in her survey of young scientists.

In analyzing how we got to this place, Turkle drew on a thinker far removed from Silicon Valley: T. S. Eliot. Turkle was interested in Eliot's grandiose but convincing theory about how poetry changed between the Elizabethan era and the eighteenth century, laid out in his essay "The Metaphysical Poets."

In this essay, it's clear that Eliot loves John Donne and less-famous Elizabethan/Jacobean English poets such as Bishop King. He notes that the term *metaphysical* has been applied to them throughout the centuries with a tinge of condescension; they've been categorized as "analytical" because they have a tendency to employ complicated metaphors in service of philosophical musing. Eliot quotes Donne's "A Valediction of Weeping":

> *On a round ball*
> *A workeman that hath copies by, can lay*
> *An Europe, Afrique, and an Asia.*
> *And quickly make that, which was nothing, All,*
> > *So doth each teare,*
> > *Which thee doth weare,*

*A globe, yea world by that impression grow,*
*Till thy tears mixt with mine doe overflow*
*This world, by waters sent from thee, my*
　　*heaven dissolved so.*

Eliot admires the way Donne goes beyond pointing out similarities between things. After all, most of us who wrote poetry in tenth grade were excited to discover there were many ways in which lovers' souls could be compared to owls attempting to locate each other through song in a snowy wood. Donne's work is typical of the best Elizabethan poetry in that it guides the reader along an alpine path of thought with simple words and structurally complex sentences. A ball becomes a world, which becomes a tear, which becomes a world again, which becomes a flood that dissolves heaven—all in two sentences, the latter of which contains nine commas.

This kind of writing, Eliot argues, has been out of fashion among English poets for hundreds of years. He compares nineteenth-century poets such as Tennyson unfavorably to Donne and his contemporaries:

> The difference is not a simple difference of degree between poets. It is something which had happened to the mind of England between the time of Donne or Lord Herbert of Cherbury and the time of Tennyson and Browning; it is the difference between the intellectual poet and the reflective poet. Tennyson and Browning are poets, and they think; but they do not feel their thought as immediately as the odour of a rose.

A poet feeling his thought as immediately as the odor of a rose: what an alien concept in an age in which poetry is closely affiliated with swooning and adolescence. For Donne and his contemporaries, says Eliot, *thinking* and *feeling* were seamlessly integrated. The poets who came after them "revolted against the ratiocinative, the descriptive; they thought and felt by fits, unbalanced; they reflected." This is a development Eliot finds unfortunate. As an example, he quotes from Tennyson's description of an adorable family in "The Two Voices":

> *The prudent partner of his blood*
> *Leaned on him, faithful, gentle, good,*
> *Wearing the rose of womanhood.*
>
> *And in their double love secure,*
> *The little maiden walked demure,*
> *Pacing with downward eyelids pure.*
>
> *These three made unity so sweet,*
> *My frozen heart began to beat,*
> *Remembering its ancient heat.*

Whether or not you find Tennyson moving, you have to admit Eliot's point: these are lines about how watching the family makes the narrator *feel,* and that's pretty much it. There's plenty of cerebral stuff in "The Two Voices," but right here Tennyson seems only to be recording an unsurprising way of thinking about love. It succeeds in choking you up, but it doesn't seduce your brain the way it seduces your heart. More precisely, it reflects a mind-set that makes a grave distinction between brain and heart, and it courts the latter.

Donne's a more impressive poet to Eliot because it seems natural for Donne to aim at your head and your heart at the same time; or rather, it never would have occurred to Donne to make the distinction between the two. Tennyson learned the habit of making that distinction, and of aiming for the lower organ, because he was part of a poetic tradition, going back to the eighteenth century, that rebelled against the "ratiocinative." (To *ratiocinate* means to think or argue logically.) This revolt against the ratiocinative has contributed to the concept of the nerd.

People have come to believe that feeling and thinking are discrete activities. Since the Romantic era, we have been in an age in which machines have the capacity for some minimal semblance of rational thought, performing tasks that once would have been the exclusive domain of humans. Reason is no longer quintessentially human; spontaneity is. People more inclined toward logical deliberation than spontaneous expression have started to become somehow less than totally human, falling into a state of alienation from the rest of humanity, dragged into the orbit of the machine and the rational, unable to convince the rest of us to consider their emotional lives seriously. In Western literature, we see them lift from the ooze and stalk about: Mary, Tibby, and Gussie.

In *The Second Self,* Turkle writes:

> Thought and feeling are inseparable. When they are torn from their complex relationship with each other and improperly defined as mutually exclusive, the cognitive can become mere logical process, the cold, dry, and lifeless, and the affective is reduced to the visceral, the primitive, and the unanalyzable.

The pathos of being a nerd is to feel that because you are comfortable with rational thought, you are cut off from the experience of spontaneous feelings, of romance, of nonrational connection to other people. A nerd is so often self-loathing because he accepts the thinking/feeling rift, and he knows and cares that other people accept it, too. To be a nerd is often to live with a nagging feeling of one's own incurable heartlessness.

# the word *nerd*
## and the birth and growth of the guy
## in high pants and glasses

### "there was no word for them that I can remember, but you'd spot them a mile away"

In *If I Ran the Zoo,* a 1950 children's book, Dr. Seuss drew a creature called a "nerd" that had only a grave countenance to suggest any similarity between itself and nerds as we now know them. But a year later, in 1951, an article on regional slang in the front pages of *Newsweek* described *nerd* as a Detroit term for "a drip or a square."

There were other possible origins for the word *nerd.* Mortimer Snerd was the idiot dummy who bantered with the ventriloquist Edgar Bergen when Bergen wasn't occupied with the more famous puppet Charlie McCarthy, but Snerd was stupid, not nerdy. He looked a little like Alfred E. Neuman, with buck teeth and an idiot grin.

The nerd look without the word *nerd* dates at least as far back as the Depression. In 1936, a comic-book writer and editor, Sheldon Mayer, began to publish strips about an aspiring cartoonist named Scribbly. Scribbly was not a nerd in the sense of being a greasy grind; the other kids in his class loved him because of the way he defied the teacher and got to take time off from school to work at his comic-book job. But he was a nerd in that he looked like a nerd as we think of them today: chunky glasses, buck teeth, so shrimpy he had to stand on stilts to dance with his girlfriend. His enemy and romantic rival was an athlete named Bentley.

Ten years later, there was a more fully formed nerd, still lacking the name, but in possession of most of the nerd characteristics: pedantry, attempts at using Standard English in conversation, a nasal voice similar to those of his 1980s and '90s descendents, Louis Skolnick in *Revenge of the Nerds* and Steve Urkel in *Family Matters*. This was Walter Denton, of *Our Miss Brooks,* which debuted as a CBS radio comedy in the late 1940s and made the leap to CBS television in the early 1950s. In *Our Miss Brooks,* Connie Brooks, a single, sharp-tongued high-school English teacher played by Eve Arden, catches a ride to school each day with a student, Walter, in his jalopy. One exchange:

> "*Before the hallowed walls of our beloved Madison High heaves
>     into view—*"
> "*What do you mean by 'heaves into view'?*"
> "*Well, every so often, you read about a ship that 'hove into view,'
>     doncha?*"
> "*Yes.*"
> "*Well, hove must be the past tense mustn't it? Heave, have, hove,
>     isn't it?*"

Walter wants to impress Miss Brooks with his vocabulary, but he doesn't know that *hove* is a nautical term, and he only makes things worse when he tries to conjugate *heave.* He's no substitute for a real boyfriend with a real car, and the point of his existence is to focus attention on Miss Brooks's singleness. Age difference aside, his voice, his lecturing, his longing to speak in the language of books— these leave him desexualized.

In the 1960s, the stereotype finally came together in whole. From its founding in 1952 until 1967, when it became a hippie magazine, the Rensselaer Polytechnic Institute's *Bachelor* was a consistently average triyearly college humor journal. It opened with a few pages of jokes, then moved on to a *Playboy*-inspired portfolio of portraits of women who lived near RPI in the Troy, New York, area. It devoted the middle pages to satire, sci-fi, and Salingeresque fiction, and wrapped up with parodies, cartoons, and news photos with salacious captions. Along with MIT's *Voodoo,* the *Bachelor* was a place where young engineers could publicly explore their self-loathing; it always joked about the antisocial tendencies of the student body. In November 1953, it published a single-panel cartoon by a student named Norm Kurdell that crystallized what was funny about a particular RPI type. The protagonist had glasses, bony arms, a flattop haircut, and a tie. His pickup line was unconventional; he sat beside a disinterested female and told her, "Then, you divide the square root of acceleration by the coefficient of friction, which of course gives you . . ." This was a description of sex as a mechanical process— a machine-minded person's attempt to grapple with an animal urge.

Kurdell, RPI '56, remembers the school's nerds before they had a name. "We used to comment about some guys. Their slide rule would be protected in a leather case. I'd say one out of ten guys would be walking around to class with their slide rules hanging out of their belts just like a sword—we didn't call them 'nerds,' but they were *different*. They were really into book learning and the work. There was no word for them that I can remember, but you'd spot them a mile away; I remember one time we were talking about how these guys were going to have a sword fight [with their slide rules] to see who has the answer first." Horn-rimmed glasses, Kurdell remembers, were strongly associated with this type.

Charlie Schmidt, RPI '67, distinctly remembers the moment at the institute when the word *tool* gave way to the word *nerd* as the name for this kind of student. "In the fall of '63, the word *tool,* both as a noun and a verb, was in widespread usage, with *supertool* commonly used to refer to the pocket-protector, slide-rule-on-the-belt types," he writes in an e-mail. "By the second semester, I remember starting to hear *nerd* as an alternative to *supertool*. A year (or less) later, and no one was referred to as a tool."

The word *nerd* never appears in the *Bachelors* of the early 1950s. Instead, there is a description in 1954 of the grind: "He is dressed in rumpled suntans, coat sweater, and thick glasses. Three-day beard optional at extra cost. Comes equipped with two slide rules, belt-mounted pencil sheath, and a vacuum tube handbook. Place your hand firmly on his arm, and he says, 'OK, Prof.' Complete with bookbag and sour expression." Given that the "belt-mounted pencil sheath" is an early variant on the pencil protector,[1] this is a pretty good description of the nerd. The visual image is there, and so is

1. The pencil protector was invented in 1947. Sales of pencil protectors actually peaked in the 1980s.

the category, and it suggests that the nerd inherited some of his defining traits from the grind.

The word *nerd* never appeared in the 1950s *Bachelor,* but the sounds in *nerd* were already in place. In the jokes section of a 1945 issue of *Running Light,* the magazine of RPI's naval ROTC, there's a joke that says the epitaph on the gravestone of one "Miss Abagale Snerd" reads, "Who says you can't take it with you?" Since the joke's insinuation is that the woman died an old maid, taking her virginity into the afterlife, the last name Snerd is made to suggest an unsexualized, probably unattractive person—this five years before *If I Ran the Zoo.*

Finally, in 1964, a character named Nurdly appeared in the *Bachelor,* a naïve freshman in a *West Side Story* parody about fraternity recruiting tactics. This jibes with Charlie Schmidt's memory of *nerd* becoming a popular term early that year. Later in 1964, there was another piece about rush week that mentioned one house's policy of sending all of its "nurds" out for party supplies when the potential recruits came over. In 1965, a student-made ad for class rings ran on the back cover and bore the caption "Why Are These 61 Nurds Smiling?" The image was a sea of guys in button-down shirts and chunky glasses, with unathletic builds, holding up their ring fingers to display their class rings in a kind of mass salute.

Later in 1965, a regular *Bachelor* contributor named Jack Gelb wrote a James Bond spy thriller parody called "The Wedge: The Simplest of Tools." The Wedge was a secret agent depicted in an illustration as having unkempt, stringy black hair, oversized glasses, and a button-down buttoned up too high. He carried a slide rule. A white pocket-shaped object with a *W* on it lay over his shirt pocket, possibly a pocket protector. The story told us that the

Wedge belonged to the species *"Homo nurdus extraordinaire,"* and fought evil by figuring out science problems. The 1966 sequel to the original Wedge adventure even developed a more contemporary spelling of *nurd*—it was called "The Man from N.E.R.D."

By the time the *Bachelor* printed its *The Man from U.N.C.L.E.* send-up, MIT's *Voodoo* had started using the word *nurd* in its joke pages. And the *Bachelor* writers had started to use *nerd* as a description of themselves. In an interview with the magazine's fictional mascot, Old Man Tuckit, Tuckit insulted his interviewer by calling him *"Bachelor* nerd." And an article about a trip to New York City described locals shouting to RPI men, "Hey, nurd!"

Jerry Lewis had just introduced Julius Kelp, the scientist with the bow tie, the lab coat, and the buck teeth, in *The Nutty Professor.* Released by Paramount in June 1963, the film retells Jekyll and Hyde as nerd and hipster.[2] The Technicolor makes it look like *The Wizard of Oz* viewed through dry contact lenses, and the performances are so underdirected, you can see minor characters pause to remember their lines. But the mannerisms and clothing of Julius Kelp are prescient, similar to the nerd sketches on *Saturday Night Live,* which came along thirteen years later, and *The Revenge of the Nerds,* which came along twenty-one years later, and more extreme. So extreme, in fact, that if Jim Carrey were to use them in a movie today, people would probably complain that he was making fun of people with autism. Kelp's social antennae are so useless that when the dean chews him out and asks a rhetorical question ("How long have you been at this university, Kelp?") he takes out a

---

2. Lewis also played the near-sighted son of a football hero who was so intellectual that he wore glasses as a baby in the 1951 Martin and Lewis picture *That's My Boy.*

pocket watch and begins to calculate the answer down to the minute. His voice is so unaffectedly nasal and flat, his posture so unathletic and unimposing, that he bears a greater resemblance to Dustin Hoffman in *Rain Man* than to Louis Skolnick in *Revenge*. But the movie never uses the word *nerd*. The earliest instance I could find of a connection between the visual image Lewis put on the big screen and the word for that image—*nurd/nerd*—is in the *Bachelor* magazine, almost immediately after the *The Nutty Professor*'s release. Eleven years pass between the *Bachelor*'s 1965 use of the complete nerd image (in "The Wedge") and the first *Saturday Night Live* nerd sketches starring Bill Murray and Gilda Radner, but the visual template is basically unchanged.

## beatts and shuster birth todd and lisa

The first *Saturday Night Live* nerds sketch was written by Rosie Shuster and Anne Beatts shortly after the appearance of Elvis Costello as the musical guest on December 17, 1977. What took place that night is now a famous performance. Substituting for the Sex Pistols, who'd canceled, Costello started to play his midtempo single "Less Than Zero," then turned to his band, spastically waving his arms, and commanded them to stop. "I'm sorry, ladies and gentlemen," he mumbled into the microphone. "There's no reason to play that song." He spun around and ordered his band to play "Radio Radio," his anti-mass-media anthem, and they managed to swing despite playing very fast. The cameras never went off; it was a power-of-live-television, bite-the-hand-that-feeds-you moment. It was not an easy turnaround for Lorne Michaels, the show's executive producer. One of the memorable aspects of the experience, for Beatts, was watching Michaels have a "brain melt."

But it was before Costello's performance, during the period Costello hung out in the studio in his signature outfit of short pants and jacket and glasses, that Beatts was struck by a profundity: "This isn't punk rock," she thought to herself. "This is nerd rock."

Born Declan MacManus, the real person behind the Elvis Costello performance was not even remotely a nerd. The son of hip parents—a jazz musician and a record store manager—he'd spent the early to mid-1970s wearing wire-rimmed Lennon glasses and medium-length hair, listening to The Band, Neil Young, and Van Morrison, working unskilled computer-operation jobs (he had no interest or ability in computer programming), and playing in pub bands. It was when he was twenty-two, after he'd signed with Stiff Records, that he and the label pieced together his look—the huge Buddy Holly glasses, the cuffed jeans, the thrift-store jacket. It was a look that fit both the punk era and the emotional state that emerged in his songs and live performances—self-loathing, fear of intimacy, alienation. Declan MacManus wasn't a nerd.[3] Elvis Costello was.[4]

The year Beatts was tormented for her association with her classmate Marshall and for her prepubescent body and undergarments, her future writing partner, Rosie Shuster, was suffering similarly, young for her class, still flat-chested, at Forest Hill Collegiate Institute Junior High in Toronto. But she did have one quality she could privately lord over her classmates: her father was a comedian.

Frank Shuster was half of the Canadian comedy duo called

3. Graeme Thomson, *Complicated Shadows: The Life and Music of Elvis Costello.*
4. In the early 1980s Costello considered renaming himself Napoleon Dynamite, but the creators of the hit nerd-love film of the same name deny his would-be alias was an influence.

Wayne and Shuster. His cousin was Joe Shuster, one of Superman's cocreators, and in her childhood, Rosie had been fascinated by Clark Kent's glasses and their ability to sap his divine strength. More importantly, a life in comedy meant that Frank Shuster nodded, rather than laughed, at jokes that worked. Rosie developed a set of criteria for what constituted an effective joke and what did not, and given her present circumstances—junior high—there was ample opportunity to observe the funniness of others' attempts to be funny.

"The so-called sense of humor of nerdy kids really intrigued me," says Shuster. She particularly relished kids who were "desperate for some entrée into popular society," whose jokes were a way of saying, "Now do you love me?" One Hungarian boy, "in danger of becoming one of the Czech brothers [*SNL*'s 'Wild and Crazy Guys']," had developed a large repertoire: "'Let's not and say we did,' 'That's so funny I forgot to laugh.' 'Not!' If somebody's fly was open, he would say, 'What do birds do?' [Birds fly.]"

Then there was a girl at Forest Hill Collegiate who didn't joke at all. "She was a brainy girl, smart and got no credit for it at all. She wore crinolines, and when they stuck out from beneath her dress, they [nerdy tormentors] would say, 'It's snowing down south?'" Shuster empathized; her mother bought all her clothes.

The dynamic of the inept sadist who thought "It's snowing down south" would be his ticket to popularity and the girl dressed by her mother was the foundation for Todd and Lisa, the nerds. They were born in a sketch written by Beatts and Shuster; inspired by Beatts's Costello revelation, the sketch was called "Nerd Rock."

The nerds had cut a record called *Desperately Trying to Be Liked,* and there were songs like "I Can't Help It If I Have Egg Salad on My Retainer," and they tried unsuccessfully to give away copies for free. John Belushi would play Todd, and Gilda Radner was the obvious choice for Lisa. Radner's adolescence was not utterly unlike Lisa's; "I am the clothes my mother made me wear" was the way she described her passage into womanhood.

When Beatts and Shuster pitched this sketch, "it wasn't a hit in the room," Beatts recalls.

"You can't do nerds," she recalls Dan Aykroyd saying. "That's *Laverne & Shirley*."

This was a reference to the way the two title characters on that show used the word to describe Squiggy, a character who was a shlubby greaser rather than an actual nerd as we understand nerds today. (Fonzie also threw around *nerd* in *Happy Days* as a term of derision.) More problematically, says Beatts, "Belushi wouldn't do it because he didn't like me and Rosie."

Belushi had been the first choice for Beatts because of a character he'd played in a *National Lampoon* radio sketch called "Fifteen-Year-Old Perfect Master," a teenage Maharishi-like spiritual leader who spoke in a nasal nerd voice. When Belushi refused to act in the sketch, Bill Murray was cast as Todd, an auspicious choice. Beatts and Shuster never would have written a character who got called "pizza face" for Murray because of their sensitivity to his acne scars, but he quickly took the role. An even more important twist of fate was the on-again, off-again relationship between Murray and Radner.

"Todd and Lisa ended up mirroring [Murray and Radner's] relationship in a sick way," remembers Beatts. "Billy used to leave her messages saying, 'Todd called.' Billy had this girlfriend who he ended up marrying. She was his high-school sweetheart, Mickey Kelly, from Chicago. And when Gilda would laugh louder at all of his sketches when they were being read, you knew that they [Gilda and Bill] were together. But I think that mild sadism of Todd toward Lisa was a reflection of the dynamic of their relationship."

It didn't hurt that Murray was hungry to stake out a reputation. "Bill was the new guy who replaced Chevy in the second half of the second year. So as a consequence, he maybe more than John or Dan was looking for some roles that would define him. And it was a hit for him."

Despite Aykroyd's concern, in neither *Happy Days* nor *Laverne* nor anywhere else on TV had the nerd prototype we know today been mapped in so much detail. Beatts and Shuster had a clear sense of what a nerd dressed like from their own high-school experiences—Beatts hadn't forgotten the column that got her thrown off the newspaper—and worked closely with the show's costume designer, Franne Lee.

"Me and Rosie designed the look," Beatts tells me. "Then the wardrobe department would always be on the lookout for items of nerdiness. Gilda contributed that Lisa should always have a Kleenex sticking out of the sleeve of her sweater."

"Effluvia," adds Shuster, "was part of the nerd syndrome. A lack of smooth functioning of the endocrine system."

"Lisa Loopner[5] was definitely Jewish," says Beatts. "Her adulation of Marvin Hamlisch, her obsession with *The Way We Were*,[6] suggested Jewishness."

Shuster isn't so sure. "Loopner was a Jewishing of *Loop,* but there was no way Jane Curtin"—who played Mrs. Loopner, Lisa's mom—"was Jewish." The sex advice Mrs. Loopner gave to Lisa

---

5. Beatts recalls the spelling as "Lupner," but "Loopner" is how the name usually appears in print.
6. The love story starring Barbra Streisand and Robert Redford.

consisted mostly of an extended analogy between the act and the making of egg salad.

Written for an episode with Steve Martin as the host, "Nerd Rock" was canceled but the first nerd sketch aired three weeks later, with Bill Murray playing Todd.[7] Radner played Lisa, according to plan. The audience reaction was positive. Fan mail trickled in, and a year later one of Beatts's friends came to her with a *New York Times* clipping: the *Scribner-Bantam English Dictionary* was creating a *nerd* entry.

Elvis Costello and Stiff Records had picked up on a visual type that had been crystallizing in places like the *Bachelor* for the past fifteen years, and Shuster, Beatts, Radner, and Murray were the conduit to the rest of pop culture. *Revenge of the Nerds, Napoleon Dynamite,* Urkel: these are the children of Loopner.

## realistic nerds get five minutes on TV, 1999

Garth Ancier, the head of NBC, delivered a blunt diagnosis to the producers of *Freaks and Geeks,* a critically acclaimed hour-long drama about high-school outcasts: "There are no victories in this show."

At thirty-six, Ancier was the same age as Paul Feig, the actor/filmmaker who'd written the *Freaks and Geeks* pilot spec.[8] The problem, it became clear, was that Feig and Ancier differed on what

---

7. Todd's original last name was LaBounta; it was made up by Al Franken and Tom Davis, who wrote one nerd sketch, provoking Beatts to tell them to lay off her idea. A high-school classmate of Davis's whose last name was LaBounta then threatened to sue, so Todd's surname was changed to Di-LaMuca.

8. A *pilot* is the first episode of a TV series, written to sell a hypothetical show to a production company and/or network, and a *spec* is any script written without a buyer in place.

a victory was, and certain of the nation's Nielsen families were with Ancier. In a "show bible," a set of guidelines for the writing staff not unlike a Dungeon Master's Guide in its lists of character traits and backdrops available for use, Feig wrote, in boldface, "There are generally never any big victories at the end of each show . . . Victories are only based on mutual acknowledgment and the agreement to be tolerant of the other person's quest for self-preservation."

Feig recalls that Ancier cited an episode in which Sam, an amiable but fingernails-against-chalkboard-level-of-awkwardness nerd, finally scores a date with an older girl. When things start to go well, the girl tells Sam, "I like hanging out with you because you remind me of my sister." Probably—Ancier felt—there were more efficient ways to seduce a prime-time audience. (The lynchpin of NBC's fall 1998 lineup was a drama about oil money called *Titans*.)

When he was visited by the first musings that led to *Freaks and Geeks*, Feig was casting about for a home for a shoestring movie he'd directed himself, *Life Sold Separately*, the story of four strangers who meet in a field.

"Over the course of the next year, I was out on the road trying to sell this movie and couldn't get work and couldn't get distribution, and I thought, 'I've got to write something while I'm out here,'" recalls Feig. "I had this notion that it was going to be a high-school show acted by adults."

The adults-playing-kids scenario was to be a satirical inversion of other high-school dramas, which tend to depict teenagers acting like grown-ups, speaking grown-up lines, and leading prodigiously active love lives. But Feig changed his mind and decided to write a realistic drama that would, instead of mocking high-school shows, "right the record."

Feig wrote on the road during two desperate weeks of driving around the Midwest with *Life Sold Separately* in the trunk, trying to drum up support for the film in local theaters. He came home with a script about the suburban Midwest (Feig grew up outside Detroit, so the road trip was not his first exposure) and endurance under circumstances that erode dignity and idealism. "For most of us, high school was about trying to get through each day without getting beaten up or humiliated," he wrote in the bible. "High school was about survival."

When his wife, Laurie, a talent manager, read the script, she suggested he send it to Judd Apatow, a friend of Feig's from his stand-up days who'd become sought-after in the early 1990s after executive producing *The Ben Stiller Show* and *The Larry Sanders Show* (he's now most famous for *The 40-Year-Old Virgin* and *Knocked Up*). When Apatow had landed a development deal with DreamWorks TV, he'd asked Feig for scripts.

Twelve hours later Apatow left a message saying he wanted to buy *Freaks and Geeks* and sell it to DreamWorks.[9] DreamWorks, recalls Feig, was "well into it." NBC execs, for their part, "were looking for a high-school show and weren't happy with the high-school shows they'd developed."

This bargaining position allowed for certain unusual casting decisions: "We made a pact," says Feig, "that there was no way they were going to force me to cast it with handsome kids."

Some of the characters did, in the end, come to life as pretty people—the show was a break for James Franco, Busy Phillips, and

9. The path from pilot spec to televised show generally runs: writer (Feig) to production company (Apatow Productions) to studio (DreamWorks TV) to network (NBC).

Linda Cardellini. But the three nerd boys at the heart of half the story lines looked like nerd boys. These were the characters most alien to American network television.

When Feig was in high school, from 1976 to 1980, *nerd* was a relatively new term and still funny—he had the *National Lampoon* foldout poster "Are You A Nerd?" on his bedroom wall (an anatomical breakdown of a nerd, it was almost used as a prop in one of the geeks' bedrooms, but Laurie Feig mistakenly threw it out before it could find immortality there). When Feig invented the name for the show, he was self-conscious about a historical inaccuracy; in 1980, when the show takes place, the word was *nerd,* and *geek* hadn't become popular yet. Beatts and Shuster's *SNL* sketches were still the most influential portrait.

One way of describing Feig's achievement with the *Freaks and Geeks* nerd characters Sam Weir and Neal Schweiber is to say that he took Lisa Loopner and Todd DiLaMuca and dramatically complicated them. Sam is tiny, dreamy, demure, and romantic, "not a nerd in the Hollywood sense," as Feig wrote in his show bible. "He doesn't wear glasses with tape in the middle or snort when he laughs. He's not even into computer programming." However, "He and his friends are a bit backward and immature. They're obsessed with things like *Monty Python,* Warner Bros. cartoons and *Star Wars.*" Neal—Todd to Sam's Lisa—is "weirdly confident" (show bible again) for a tiny hairy guy, and his confidence allows him to deliver loud, frequent borscht belt jokes. While Todd wears clothes his mom buys, Neal considers himself an expert critic of dress. But unlike Todd and Lisa, they pine for people who live outside their nerd world. Sam falls for a popular alpha-girl; Neal thinks he's the one who can "save" Lindsay, Sam's older sister, from the stoner crowd. Like most people we call nerds, they're not the embodiment of a perfect Platonic nerdiness, like Todd and Lisa. They're part nerd, and being part nerd generally means wanting people who are non-nerds, but being addicted to nerd pleasures.

In addition to all this, Sam and Neal are autobiographical vessels. "Sam is totally me," Feig told me, "and Judd is more Neal Schweiber." They resonate with other boys who went into Feig and Apatow's business; when Feig wrote Steven Spielberg to thank DreamWorks for producing *Freaks and Geeks,* Spielberg wrote back a short letter stating, "I am a fan and a geek and proud of both those affiliations." (Feig has the letter framed on the wall of his office.)

But the contribution Feig made to TV history wasn't his decision to write about geeks instead of more conventional heroes. His contribution (an un-Spielbergian one) was to reject the idea of heroes. The people who are admirable to most of fictional Chippewa, Michigan—the jock, the cheerleader, the James Dean rebel boy—are variously abusive or insensitive toward the main characters in *Freaks and Geeks*. The eponymous groups aren't heroic either; they're often escapist, stunted, and preoccupied with themselves to the point of being unable to help others. The show took a network audience accustomed to hot people solving problems and instead asked them to find beauty in unhot people learning to deal with the insolubility of problems. This movement—from hero worship to an acceptance that all there is to like in this world is people as degraded as yourself—is a path to adulthood I took along with my friends through adolescence.

Of course, there are other ways to grow up. When I ask Feig why the jocks in *Freaks and Geeks* hate the nerds, he directs my attention to the world of adults. "Guys like that just seem to hate guys like us, and I honestly see the battle between Democrat and

Republican, liberal and conservative, as the exact same dynamic—there's a group of people in this world that don't like conflict and care about what other people are going through, and then there's this other group of people in the world who hate that. 'Suck it up, man, we're not coddling you, take care of yourself, what's your problem?' It's jocks versus geeks, and I've always referred to life as perpetual high school because it never stops."

# effeminate jewish grinds,
# cyborg asians

### the racism chart

This is my theory about contemporary Western racism and how it relates to the concepts of the jock and the nerd:

| REALLY SENSUAL | | HUMAN | | NOT SENSUAL |
|---|---|---|---|---|
| Animals | Africans | Europeans | Asians | Machines |
| | jocks | | nerds | |

In this model,[1] nerds are people who have been sucked into the orbit of the machine and sapped of human emotion. Asians are more machinelike (industrious, asexual) than whites by cultural in-

---

1. This semieugenic worldview can also be an ice-breaking party game. Players enumerate their common friends and acquaintances, including those in the room, and decide who is most machine, who is most animal, and where others fall on the machine-animal spectrum.

heritance and/or genetic predisposition. Therefore, Asians tend to be nerds.

Racism can be lumped grossly into "primitivist racism" and "orientalist racism." [2] The former casts a given race as too sensual, too tied to the land, too emotional, too animal. The latter casts a given race as too abstract, too contemplative, cut off from the sensual world. Primitivist racism tends to target Africans and orientalist racism tends to target Asians and Arabs. For my racism chart, I've fused this model with Sherry Turkle's idea that the machine age, especially the computer, has caused modern educated humans to define what is human as "emotional," in contrast to thinking machines, instead of just defining what is human as "rational," in contrast to other animals. Orientalist racism has become so intertwined with the popular image of nerds that nerds express an identification with Asian cultures as a way of asserting their nerdiness. (More on that later.)

Orientalist and primitivist racism have been around for a long time. In 1776, J. R. Blumenbach, a German naturalist, theorized that human beings originated as Caucasians, so named because of their supposed proximity to the Caucasus Mountains, and underwent a degeneration into Asians, the middle rung of the ladder, and then Africans, the bottom. In modern American racist literature, this Asian race became the "mongoloid race," and was generally defined in contrast to "Nordic stock." The progressive-era American

2. *Orientalist* here is defined differently from *orientalist* in Edward Said's famous 1978 book *Orientalism*. Said used the word to describe a colonialist view of all non-Western peoples as childlike and irrational. My concept of orientalist racism and how it relates to nerds comes from a 2002 paper by the Rensselaer Polytechnic Institute professor Ron Eglash, "Race, Sex and Nerds: From Black Geeks to Asian-American Hipsters."

racialist Madison Grant argued in his 1916 book *The Passing of the Great Race* that Nordics, the "master race," were distinguished because they

> are all over the world, a race of soldiers, sailors, adventurers and explorers, but above all, of rulers, organizers and aristocrats . . . The Nordic race is domineering, individualistic, self-reliant and jealous of their personal freedom both in political and religious systems and as a result they are usually Protestant. Chivalry and knighthood and their still surviving but greatly impaired counterparts are peculiarly Nordic traits, and feudalism, class distinctions and race-pride among Europeans are traceable for the most part to the north.

Nordics, crucially, were not the smartest race in Grant's pseudoscience, just the most noble.

> The mental characteristics of the Mediterranean race are well known and this race, while inferior in bodily stamina to both the Nordic and the Alpine, is probably the superior of both, certainly of the Alpines, in intellectual attainments. In the field of art, its superiority to both the other European races is unquestioned . . .

He went on to note that

> Negroes have demonstrated throughout recorded time that they are a stationary species, and that they

do not possess the potentiality of progress or initiative from within. Progress from self-impulse must not be confounded with mimicry or with progress imposed from without by social pressure, or by the slavers' lash.

As for the Negro's opposite: "the Polish Jew, . . . dwarf stature, peculiar mentality, and ruthless concentration on self-interest."

Grant's emphasis on the courageous disposition of the Nordic nicely accommodated the centuries-old commonplace in English literature that Jews shied from physical confrontation (while white supremacists historically disagree about what Nordics are, they generally agree that Nordics are not Jews). Still, modern Western anti-Semitism has been so varied that it's hard to locate Jews on the animal-machine racism chart. Voltaire attacked the Jews for being too devout and insufficiently rational. The eighteenth-, nineteenth-, and twentieth-century Romantic nationalists attacked Jews for being excessively rational, lacking the spiritual attachment to a particular land necessary to create a strong, unified country. A tradition of German anti-Semitism bestialized Jews, depicting them as animals with claws, and in eighteenth-century English anti-Semitic caricature, Jews were shown as having a secret lust for all things porcine, which resulted in sodomy with pigs. Part of Nazi ideology was that Jews were sexual predators who threatened the purity of the Aryan gene pool by violating pure-blooded women. In America, however, the nonsensual, nonearthy Asians and Jews have generally stood on one side of a gallery of racial stereotypes, while American Indians and other perceived "primitives" have stood on the other.

■

"We are submerged beneath a conquest so complete that the very name of us means something not ourselves . . . I feel as I should think an Indian might feel, in the face of ourselves that were," wrote a WASP named Barrett Wendell, a Harvard professor whose lifetime, 1855–1921, corresponded with a flood of immigration that created intense resentment. The year Wendell was born, Charles DeLong, a white lawyer, tax collector, and Democratic politician in California, wrote in his journal of a ritual thought to recall the scalpings that American Indians visited on settlers. "Started with Dick Wade and Bob Moulthrop collecting: supper at Hesse's Crossing went down the river in the night collected all the way had a great time, Chinamen tails cut off"—he'd run amok among the Chinese immigrants, seized them, and lopped off their braided ponytails, or "queues."

As the historian Robert G. Lee put it in his book *Orientals,* "The taking of 'scalps' enabled white workingmen to relive an imagined earlier pre-industrial past." Cheap Chinese immigrant labor was thought to feed the new industrial capitalism that was turning white working-class artisans into factory laborers, and the subservience to mechanized, repetitive work that the factory demanded. The white man could see himself as the inheritor of the Indian's physical bravado and connection to the soil, because the Chinese were thought of as peacefully submitting to industrial employers. They represented the submissive, repetitive work life of the future.

The minstrel shows of the time used not only the famous Zip Coon and Jim Crow characters, but also a figure called John Chinaman. The comical vices of Zip Coon were his laziness and trickery, but the deficiency of John Chinaman was that he couldn't hold on to his girlfriend so long as a white man wanted to take her.

The minstrel song "Big Long John" described an Indian taking the title character's scalp along with his braid—as the song put it, "he died from loss of his queue."

The Asian population of the United States was small—not much more than 1 million people—until the immigration act of 1965, which allowed for renewed migration from East and South Asian countries, a flow of new citizens composed largely of members of the professional classes. Because the act's policies made immigration much easier for educated families, and because many of those first educated immigrant parents found themselves holding more menial jobs in the United States than the ones they'd held in their native countries, there was often an unusual degree of pressure on their children to enter the professions in America, and by the early 1980s Asian-Americans constituted a much larger percentage of the student bodies at top colleges than they did in the population in general. *Time* heralded the new "Asian-American Whiz Kids."[3]

One consequence of this mildly threatening vision of Asians was that John Chinaman and Big Long John survived in spirit, emerging largely intact in *Sixteen Candles,* John Hughes's 1984 teen comedy, as Long Duk Dong. Dong shared with John Chinaman the problem of being attracted to women who would rather be with white men. In a John Chinaman minstrel song, John described taking a walk and coming back to find his girlfriend had been seduced by his white friend, Mose, a stock character in minstrel shows who stood for the working-class white man. The tone of John Chinaman's song shares with Long Duk Dong's remarks a cheerful industriousness and social ineptitude. In *Sixteen Candles,*

3. Masi Oka, currently a star of NBC's drama *Heroes,* was one of the bespectacled Asian children who appeared on *Time*'s cover in 1986.

Molly Ringwald's parents remind her that Long Duk Dong excels at doing chores. Long Duk Dong stares at her with longing, and, famously, dangles upside down from the top of a bunk bed to call her, in inflectionless speech, his face all dazed oblivion, "hot stuff."

Molly Ringwald hates Long Duk Dong because he doesn't realize he's a disgusting sexual prospect, and her parents like him because he's hardworking and inoffensive. And inoffensiveness is the link between the stereotypes of the Chinese-Americans who settled on the Pacific Coast in the nineteenth century and Romantic-era stereotypes of Jews popular in England and America. The eighteenth-century minister of Parliament James Howell described Jews as "the most timorous people on earth, and so utterly incapable of Arms, for they are neither Soldiers nor Slaves: and thus their Pusillanimity and Cowardice . . . may be imputed to their various thraldoms, contempt and poverty, which hath cow'd and dastardized their courage." The writer Tobias Smollett felt they were "the least of any people . . . addicted to military life." "They are rarely to be found engaged in any of the personal outrages that are so common in the metropolis," observed one English writer of Jews in 1842. "And even in the very few instances in which the name of a Jew is to be found mixed up in any scuffle or affray that takes place, it will almost always be found that he is not the aggressor. A Jew is a singularly quiet, inoffensive member of society." In 1871, Mark Twain published an article on the Chinatowns in West Coast cities called "The Gentle, Inoffensive Chinese." "A disorderly Chinaman is rare, and a lazy one does not exist," he wrote. "Chinamen make good house-servants, being quick, obedient, patient, quick to learn, and tirelessly industrious." It wasn't until these two groups began their initiations into the schools of the American upper middle class that they could acquire reputations as "grind" cultures—but both much earlier acquired reputations for meekness and physical restraint.

In the case of Jews, a certain protonerdiness might have started much, much earlier. Because Jews were required by doctrine to read the Torah four times a week, Jews tended to learn to read at a much higher rate than other ethnic groups in the centuries just after Christ. As a consequence they all but abandoned farming much earlier than the rest of humanity began to drift away from agriculture—they began the process around AD 200, and by AD 700 about 90 percent of Jews had moved into other trades, long before the medieval laws that forbade Jewish farming. The Berkeley professor Daniel Boyarin argued that the rabbinical culture that developed in the Roman Empire involved a version of manhood at odds with the dominant Roman one. The Roman gender constructs associated masculinity with aggression and femininity with reception, whereas one rabbinical masculine ideal was a man who read the Talmud and understood it, declining contests of strength, declining nonintellectual professions. There was some rationale, Boyarin felt, for the stereotypes of Jews that evolved in Europe. (What to the dominant culture in Europe was contemptible was to Boyarin something worth preserving.) Boyarin's intent was to show how Jews subverted gender roles, but the evidence Boyarin marshalled to illustrate his point that Western images of Jewish men often makes Jews look *nerdy,* that is, poorly equipped to handle physical confrontation, made for the abstract realms of finance and scripture. He cites a Yiddish folk song, written from the perspective of a young woman who wants a husband, that includes the line "for Holy Torah he must be fit," but no mention of any conventionally masculine qualities. An 1890 German cartoon of a Jewish boy with giant ears and spindly limbs falling off a bicycle seems to equate Jewishness with a lack of athleticism. These images suggest Jews sometimes played a role in certain popular imaginations not so different from that of today's nerd.

As a general rule, notions of ethnic identity are deployed as politically and economically expedient. The WASP establishment in the early twentieth century was confronted with a threat to its position and so created an ethnicity-informed distinction between the invading force and itself: a dichotomy between the athletic man of character and the "greasy grind." This was a precursor to the contemporary dichotomy of jock and nerd. Put another way, the nerd is the grind stripped of the immigrant/Jewish/sinister/unknown-ethnic-identity status implied in the older term. The American nerd concept contains the residue of a social strategy meant to keep immigrant overachievers at bay.

Shortly after a substantial and growing percentage of the Harvard student body came to be Jewish, administrations of Harvard, Yale, and Princeton started to equate Jewishness with what would now be described as nerdiness. Jerome Karabel's *The Chosen,* a 2005 tome on admissions policies at the three schools, found a pile of documents that made the link. After sheltering the northeastern Protestant elite from immigrants ceased to be a major priority for Harvard administrators, the Jew-grind association persisted. Wilbur Bender, who was chairman of Harvard's Committee on Admission from 1952 to 1960, helped transform Harvard from a school for privileged New England boys into a more national, meritocratic institution. Still, he observed "there is a high percentage of Jewish boys" among the "intellectual, musical or aesthetic individuals . . . coming largely from metropolitan centers," which included "some of our most unattractive and undesirable ones, the effeminates, the precious and affected, the unstable." Bender painted Jews as effete intellectuals, not as nerds per se. But in his status on campus, his combination of intellectual power and social powerlessness, Bender's Jew was an ancestor of the nerd.

## when japan was about to
## put robots in charge of america

When William Gibson wrote the sci-fi novel *Neuromancer* in the early 1980s, he designed a seductive, nightmarish future. For nerds, who were increasingly visible in pop culture in 1984, the year of the book's publication, it was a flag to rally around, a fantasy in which hackers wielded enormous power and the world was run less by governments than by technologically advanced corporations. The most powerful of those corporations in *Neuromancer* were Japanese, and the novel reflected the 1980s anxiety about Japan's tech-fueled economic ascendancy. For some, a Japan-dominated future was a worst-case scenario; for nerds it held a certain romance.

Nerds developed a fascination with Japanese pop culture in the 1980s. There was something about postwar Japan itself that seemed nerdy—the cultural emphasis on order, the industriousness coupled with military helplessness, the obsessively detailed science-fiction cartoons that enacted fantasies of military domination and spectacular revenge (the resolutions of "Japanimation" movies often incorporated nuclear bombs, sometimes dropped on America). Japan, like a nerd boy rendered as a nation, was getting rich, still impotent, still vengeful, obsessed, like Victor Frankenstein, with the machines that would give it power.

The scholar Stephen Beard once described *Neuromancer* and

Ridley Scott's cyborg noir film *Blade Runner* as contributing to the "re-invention of Japan as a land of high-tech enchantment," with "manga, techno-porn, high-density urbanism, mobile fashion, hyper-violent movies, video-phones, fax cameras, hand-held televisions, video-games, disposable buildings, even a new breed of 'radically bored' teen information junkies, otaku, who shun body contact and spend all their waking hours gathering data on the most trivial bits of media." As Kevin Robins and David Morley put it in their essay "Techno-Orientalism," "These kids are imagined as people mutating into machines; they represent a kind of cybernetic mode of being for the future."

Machinelike, body-contact-shunning kids are nerds, and the myth of Japan as the nerd nation, rising from the rubble of Fat Man and Little Boy to take over the world through its technological schemes, helped cement an association in American pop culture between nerdiness and Asians. Non-Asian nerds developed an aesthetic built around Japanese pop culture. When I was in tenth grade, my friend Nick, who owned a LaserDisc player—tomorrow's technology—would throw sleepovers at his house where three of us would sit watching anime (Japanese cartoons) all night. The animes weren't so different from American action movies in terms of plot and dialogue; the splatter had a certain extra Jackson Pollock kick, but that was the extent of it. What was important to us was the sense of being allied with Japan, throwing in our lot with the country that embraced machines and the future with comical enthusiasm. We watched with both condescension and admiration; the cartoons were inadvertently funny, but they were also profound (we thought), offering a glimpse into another country that was threatening to overtake our own in international influence. We knew that Japan was important in *Neuromancer* and *Blade Runner* and that Japan was important to people who listened to techno, and that they were "totally taking over." That was all we needed to feel we were lodging some kind of protest, or at least forming some kind of outlaw band, that stood against the norms of America. People who believed in America were presumed to be watching something else.

In both *Blade Runner* and *Neuromancer,* the spread of Asian corporate power coincides with an increased presence of creatures who are part human and part machine. *Blade Runner*'s "replicants" are genetically engineered androids, and are therefore, like Frankenstein's creature, the product of new technology but not themselves machines. As Lee writes in *Orientals,* they have much in common with the Asians who fill the streets of crowded downtown Los Angeles in the film's vision of the future, and speak a hybrid language the antihero calls "gutter talk." The replicants are advertised as tireless labor, and are trying to pass for human (the job of the "blade runner" antihero is to track down a group who are trying to reprogram a feature of their internal composition that limits their lives to four years). It's their eyes that give them away as part machine (instead of being "slanted," they emit a very faint glow). In *Neuromancer,* the hero, Case, has been injected with a debilitating myotoxin by Japanese mafia guys—Yakuza—that prevents him from accessing cyberspace. He's recruited by a cyborg, Molly, to help her complete a mission that involves helping two artificial intelligence entities merge. Case, we read, "had always taken it for granted that the real bosses, the king-pins in a given industry, would be both more and less than *people.* He'd seen it in the men who crippled him in Memphis . . . He'd always imagined it as a gradual and willing accommodation of the machine, the system, the parent organism." This is the way of things in a future dominated by the Japanese—governments are less powerful in the world of *Neuromancer* than the Mitsubishi Bank of America, and the multinational corporations called zaibatsus that have "attained a kind of immortality . . . You couldn't kill a zaibatsu by assassinating a dozen key executives; there were others waiting to step up the ladder, assume the vacated position, access the vast banks of corporate memory." In these Japanese multinationals, the individual is subsumed into a machinelike order with machine memory at its essence, and in a world dominated by Japanese multinationals, humans are forced or inclined to become tied to the machine. The cruelty of the nerve poison the Yakuza give to Case is that it prevents him from making the man-machine bond.

The cruelty in *Blade Runner* is the mistreatment of the replicants, who can only be distinguished from humans through long "empathy tests" that evaluate how the pupils of their eyes react to emotionally stimulating questions.[4] At the end of the director's cut, Deckard, the Harrison Ford "blade runner" character, learns that he is a replicant; since replicants are programmed to have extensive memories of childhood and every other phase of life, it's easy for many of them to believe that they are normal humans, even though they aren't designed to last more than four years (they might develop their own emotions in potentially dangerous and unproductive ways, if given a chance to mature). The movie is at pains to show how human they are. They mourn one another's deaths, they fall in love, they experience disillusionment and rage. There is a parallel between the suffering of the replicants and the suffering that Sherry Turkle described in *The Second Self*; they are obliged to

4. See my Autism Spectrum chapter for more on connections between nerdiness and struggles to attain normal levels of empathy.

prove that their affiliation with machines hasn't robbed them of emotional lives. Trying to convince a replicant scientist to help her get an audience with the scientist who knows best how to program her, one replicant, Pris, evokes an Enlightenment idea: "I think therefore I am." This was the idea of being human that originated in a time when to be human was to be more rational than an animal. In a machine age threatened with teeming hordes of inexpressive humans in constant entanglement with machines and computer technology, the human has become the unmachine. The replicants suffer the ways nerds suffer.

## the 1980s

| Nerds | | Jocks and preppies |
|---|---|---|
| Japan | | America |
| Technology | | Physical strength |
| Reason and organization | | Intuition and animal instinct |
| | vs. | |
| Stiff | | Cool |
| Might dominate in the future | | Dominant now |
| Not sexy | | Sexy |
| Straightforward communication | | Barely speaks, uses innuendo, irony |

The most cathartic event in *Rambo: First Blood Part II* is the "arrrgh" moment in which Rambo destroys a Vietnamese prison camp by firing missiles from a captured helicopter, but the second most cathartic is the moment when Rambo returns to his American base in Southeast Asia and, without provocation, guns down a row of computers. The computers hiss and shoot sparks. They are the tools of Murdock, a spineless bureaucrat who sends Rambo on a mission to photograph POWs in Vietnam but wants Rambo to find none so that accord between America and Vietnam will prevail. As Trautman, Rambo's ally in the military establishment, puts it to Murdock, nobody knows the dirty secrets but "you and your computers, and you can reprogram that." Earlier on, Murdock advises Rambo to let technology do the fighting for him on his mission. "The mind is the best weapon," Rambo replies, and events bear out that hypothesis: Rambo takes out hordes of lumpen Vietnamese with a knife and a bow and arrow, fighting like a supernatural American Indian. (Rambo is half Indian and half German, "a hell of a combination.") He says "aargh" quite a bit. This is a way of setting up Rambo as an antinerd.

"Aargh" and its variants were Mel Gibson's specialty throughout a long, productive period starting with *Lethal Weapon* and climaxing with *Braveheart,* in which, tortured in a public square, he shouted, "Freedom!"[5] Arnold Schwarzenegger's first several forays into dialogue in 1982's *Conan the Barbarian* are all "aaaaaarghs"— when he first opens his mouth he's a pit fighter, so this is understandable.

The noises in these movies are complemented by shirtlessness. Usually, clothes confer sophistication, nakedness confers vulnerability. Advertising your body implies that the brain isn't the organ that sets you apart. But one of the tricks of bodybuilding, as the historian Richard Dyer has observed, is to make a display of nakedness a display of status. A built body takes huge amounts of discipline, leisure time, and nutrition. Unlike, say, a conventionally hot woman's body, which might be the product of exercise and disci-

5. "Fucking Jew," a cry of passion directed at a niggardly but impeccably organized evil force, might be understood as an extension of this tradition.

plined eating but might be largely a gift from God, the body-built body has to be a triumph of willpower over physical anguish. It's a rich person's body.

It is in this context that the behavior of Ogre in *Revenge of the Nerds* must be interpreted. The largest and most warlike of the jocks, with a bodybuilder's physique and a barbaric haircut, it is Ogre who translates the viciousness of the jocks into speech with his cry of "Neeeeeeeerds!" a missive similar to Conan and Rambo's "aaaaaaarghs."

We hear the jocks in *Revenge of the Nerds* before we see them for the first time, and they are chanting "Ogre! Ogre!" Ogre then looks up from the anonymous victim he is dangling from the balcony, and cries "Nerds!" He begins a chant so deeply felt he doesn't know it's a chant: "Nerds! Neeeeerds! Neeeeeerds! Neeeeerds!" He has sighted Louis and Gilbert. The rest of the uniformly blond, shaggy-haired, and powerfully built jocks in turn modify their background chant from "Ogre!" to "Nerds!" and it becomes clear we are among the descendents of the Norsemen who threatened to snuff Western civilization when in their prime, and of Rambo. In *Revenge of the Nerds,* unlike *Rambo II,* the animal side is bad and the machine side is good, but the animal side in *Rambo II* resembles the animal side in *Nerds,* and the machine side in *Nerds* resembles the machine side in *Rambo II.* The animal side has hockey-player hair, muscles, a preference for sounds over speech, and Germanic looks or ancestry; the machine side has a short-sleeved shirt with a tie and hair parted at the side, and speaks clearly.

When whites fight Asians in movies, it's often a case of the physically and emotionally confrontational squaring off against the rational and soulless; in another Ridley Scott movie, *Black Rain,* the

Japanese villain puts it this way: "Music and movies are all your culture is good for . . . We make the machines!" The movie industry itself has been conceived before as the beachhead of an alien presence stealing the soul of America from within its shores; this, of course, is the concept of Jew-run Hollywood. But in the late 1980s, when Sony bought Columbia, Hollywood began to cast itself as an essentially American institution under attack from its west. Jeffrey Katzenberg wrote an editorial in *Variety* that predicted a possible mismatch between the creative culture of Hollywood and the noncreative Japanese business culture of Columbia's new owners. As it turned out, Japan didn't scoop up the movie business; at the moment Sony/Columbia is the only major Hollywood studio owned by a Japanese multinational. Moreover, Japan slipped into recession in the 1990s, and the Japanese acquisition of American companies slowed.

But the Japanese didn't cease to be a nerd ethnicity. As the cultural critic Slavoj Žižek put it, "In today's America . . . a role resembling that of the Jew is being played more and more by the Japanese. Witness the obsession of the American media with the idea that the Japanese don't know how to enjoy themselves. The reasons for Japan's increasing economic superiority over the U.S.A. is located in the somewhat mysterious fact that Japanese don't consume enough, that they accumulate too much wealth."

Writing in *Slate,* Nicholas Lemann perceived a displacement of Jews by Asians in more specific ways: "Golf and tennis are perceived by the Asian-Americans not as aspects of an ethos adapted from the British landowning classes (which is the way Jews used to perceive them), but as stuff that Jews know how to do . . . The wheel of assimilation turns inexorably: Scratching out an existence is phase one, maniacal studying is phase two, sports is phase three."

In America, the state of single-mindedly academic adolescence with no physical confrontation is something an ethnic group transcends when it becomes firmly established in the ruling class. The next phase is the well-roundedness associated with WASPs. The source of that state—of having a body that appears to have been thoughtfully designed by a benevolent God, rather than conceived as a breeding ground for viruses and a wellspring of pain—is sport. Being in the obsessively grade-grubbing phase of assimilation used to get you called a greasy grind; now it gets you called a nerd.

## the primitive boy

English professor Kenneth Kidd has argued that the concept of "feral" boys—boys raised in the wild and/or nursed by animals—has influenced modern boy-rearing in England and America. He points to how, in the late nineteenth century, the scouting movement, started by Lord Robert Baden-Powell, worked to keep boys in contact with the wild, the animal world, as described by Rudyard Kipling. Another scholar, Hugh Brogan, has described how Baden-Powell secured Kipling's permission to use material from *The Jungle Books* in his 1916 *Wolf Cub's Handbook*. The journey into manhood would not be one away from the animal and toward divine reason, as an Enlightenment thinker might have seen it, but one that preserved the animal element in a boy who was bound to grow up in a world of increasing industrialization and vanishing wilderness. When you take the wolf-boy as a model for Anglo-American youths, you can start to think of insufficiently lupine boys as deviations from the ideal.

As Kidd points out, this philosophy was in the tradition of Ralph Waldo Emerson's 1841 essay "Self-Reliance," which described the ideal American man as sharing with boys "Spontaneity or Instinct" and "intuition," an "aboriginal Self." The associative chain implied is good American= boy = savage= animalistic. Kidd also cites Charles Dudley Warner's 1877 memoir, *Being a Boy,* where Warner proclaims "everyone who is good for anything is a natural savage," with "the primal, vigorous instincts and impulses of an African savage." Given the growing imperial ambitions of both England and America, it makes sense that boys would need to become better inured against the threat of being overcivilized, and brave and tough enough to fight for the glory of the civilization in the colonial hinterlands. Kidd's theory is that the general pattern in these nineteenth-century works of "boyology" was to see normal, good boys as passing through a healthy, charming savage phase. Savages were boys, good boys were savages.

## hyperwhiteness

The speech that we associate with nerds—formal, unambiguous, cleaving to the grammar of what's often called Standard English—involves what the linguist Mary Bucholtz calls "hyperwhiteness." In studies of Bay Area high-school students who considered themselves nerds, all of whom were white or Asian, Bucholtz found that the way they spoke excluded pronunciations and slang terms that non-nerdy white classmates had appropriated from black slang. The nerds also used what linguists call "hypercorrect" pronunciations, saying words the way you would think they were pronounced if you read them without hearing them. For example, Bucholtz found that science-fiction fans and females who describe themselves as nerds are both groups that tend to create a small puff of air when they pronounce the *t* at the end of *right*. (Other California teens tend to de-emphasize that *t* or eliminate it, forming the notorious "Yeah, *ri-i'*.")

The self-described nerds favored terms of Greco-Latinate origin ("it's my observation") over those of Germanic origin ("I think"), a tendency that traditionally signifies scientific remove, literacy, and hauteur. The nerds also liked "punning, parody, word coinage," and other devices that played with "language form." Their "negative identity practices"—ways of talking they strove to avoid—included "vowel reduction, consonant-cluster simplification, and contraction," "current slang," and "nonstandard syntactic forms." In other words, your average white popular kid at the Bay Area high school used a certain amount of African-American vernacular, but the nerds avoided black slang phrases and professed an active dislike for some of them, like "kick back" and "trippin'." ("It just makes no sense to me," one of them told Bucholtz, of the dropped *g*.)

Bucholtz makes the case that the popular white kids she watched considered it part of normal whiteness to appropriate some black phrases without using *too* much black vernacular. The popular crowd that Bucholtz observed, then, had a racial logic to some degree reminiscent of the nineteenth-century nativist white men who affiliated themselves with Indians and wanted boys to experience a stage of wildness—they were holding true whiteness to contain a germ of a tough ethnicity ("scalping" of Chinamen was to them what saying "let's kick back, blood" was for the popular white boys of Bay City). Lacking the germ makes you unwhole. As Brian Eno famously put it, "What is a nerd? A nerd is a human being without enough Africa in him or her." The less famous preceding remark from Eno's 1995 interview with *Wired* is "Do you know what I hate about computers? The problem with computers is that there is not enough Africa in them.

That's why I can't use them for very long." There is an implied continuum here, with nerds and machines on one side, and Africa on the other, and people with just the right amount of Africa, like Brian Eno, in the center.

## one potentially final solution

The very nerdiest members of our society aren't particularly attached to the fate of any ethnic identity, or even to the fate of the species; they hope humans will one day generate robots with super-human intelligence, and if said robots take humans' place as masters of the earth, or even bring about our extinction, that's nature's way. Hans Moravec, founder of the robotics program at Carnegie Mellon, has written, "Robots will displace humans from essential roles. Rather quickly, they could displace us from existence. I'm not as alarmed as many by the latter possibility, since I consider these future machines our progeny . . . Like biological children of previous generations, they will embody humanity's best chance for a long-term future. It behooves us to give them every advantage and to bow out when we can no longer contribute."

Moravec, whose life's work is developing artificial intelligence, doesn't particularly care that we humans are mammals, with natural inclinations toward sexual reproduction, breast-feeding, protection of our babies, and so on. He doesn't particularly care that we're carbon-based. What makes us *us*, what makes our progeny our progeny, is intellectual functioning. Moravec's ideological ally, the MIT professor Rodney Brooks, puts it another way: "I believe myself and my children all to be mere machines. Automatons at large in the universe. Every person I meet is also a machine—a big bag of skin full of biomolecules interacting according to describable and knowable rules." If the entities best able to carry on the intellectual projects we've started are silicon-based, their logic goes, maybe we ought to get off the new road if we can't lend a hand, as Dylan put it, and accept our subjugation and possible termination gracefully.

You can't get much further from *The Passing of the Great Race,* or Geronimo, than that.

## my grandmother's prunes

There is a tradition in contemporary literature, movies, and comedy in which Jews remember the women of their families as affectionate lampreys who drain their children of dignity in the throes of some ancient hunger. I remember the grandmother on my Jewish side as being merely innocent of the concept of dignity; it didn't occur to her to take it into consideration.

"I'm trying to figure out why the toilet is clogged, Ben," she would say, lost in contemplation at the kitchen table. "And it occurred to me, that if you are not using too much toilet paper—could it be that your feces are so hard that they are clogging the toilet for that reason alone?" The most efficient way to change the subject was to assure her your feces had lately been normal. To admit hard feces would have been to risk becoming the subject of a conference. Dole prunes would be discussed on speakerphone in such tones as to suggest my grandmother had effected a feat of engineering.

"So the clogged toilet problem," she would say, chewing on an almond, "appears to have been fixed."

This is not to suggest that my grandmother was not dignified. Her dignity derived in part from her candor, but candor is not a conventional route to dignity. The dignity of the popular kids at my high school was a dignity of self-suppression. If you were going to present yourself as a leader and a sportsman, it helped to have the ability to put out of mind the baser facts of your existence. Among the Jewish women in my family, there was an ideology that might be termed antiheroism, which stood in opposition to this practice.

In a 1939 booklet, *45 Questions About the Jews,* the American anti-Semite William Dudley Pelley, founder of the fascist Silver Legion, made a similar observation about Jews: "Commonly you recognize them by the manner in which they talk. That they have no reserve, no respect for other people's privacies, and little stability of character, being arrogant and insolent one moment and fawning and wailing the next." What Pelley describes here is an indifference to dignity. What my grandmother shared with much of the nerd world was that indifference.

*part 2*

# among the nerds

# zack and jack
# and high-school debate

First, there's a solemn teenage boy: eyes downcast, marking papers with a highlighter, poker faced, adjusting glasses. Then the teenage boy is gone and a different beast takes his place; he leans a small stack of papers on a blue plastic tub full of research, using the tub as a podium, and then there is the first great rush of oxygen: *"Huuuu-uuugh . . ."*

Then the auctioneer's barrage: "The-U.S.-federal-government-should-require-high-school-students-to-participate-in-one-year-of-service-learning-through-a *huuuuughgggh* Learn-and-Serve-America-Program. *Huuuggghgh . . ."*

The gulps are so natural, so unself-conscious and efficient in the way they deliver sustenance to the lungs, that their sound is generally animal rather than distinctly human. Until you've heard someone try to wrestle so many syllables into so few seconds, you've only heard people rescued from drowning in shipwreck movies take breaths like these. They render the debater surprisingly vulnerable. Some kids have feminine gasps; others swallow, in a deep, guttural way. Some consistently let out short twin gasps—"*Hthuuuuup-hthuuuuuup.*" Some manage, through some invisible swim-team athleticism, to avoid gulps, but most gulp loud. During a lull in a debate, when the teams dig through the files in their tubs, or "oxes," you can hear the gulps in the next classroom over, through cinderblock walls.

At Georgetown Day School in Washington, DC, Zack Malitz and Jack Jenkins, a debate team from Westlake High School in Texas, are slightly bleary but ready for action. Zack walks barefoot, as is his custom, with the cuffs of his oversize jeans kissing the ground. ("Feet make the best shoes.") He has a substantial Jewfro and a goatee. He has, at seventeen, "a better grasp of postmodern Continental philosophy than some people who have PhDs," in the words of the team's DC-based former coach and supervisor for the day, Kellie Clancy.

Last night Zack and Jack arrived at Kellie's house in Washington, DC's Maryland suburbs and stayed up until the early morning running speech drills and arguing over how to make an argument about detainment without probable cause. They had just flown in from Texas carrying an easel and a choreographed bit in which Zack read from the philosopher Gilles Deleuze while Jack erected the easel and drew an abstract tree that represented the Deleuze concept at hand. Kellie persuaded them not to draw the tree, and also persuaded Jack, who had taken up a policy of not showering in order to conserve water, that as long as he was in her house, and she was paying the water bill, he might as well take a shower every day.

Zack and Kellie are, in Kellie's words, "very close." Kellie was

Zack's coach at Westlake for two years before she moved to DC, and she's only six years Zack's senior. Throughout the morning they often talk strategy, smoking cigarettes out by the Dumpster here at Georgetown Day. They tell me about Westlake.

"Basically, when Austin desegregated, the white people moved out to the hills," explains Zack, "and that's Westlake." Kellie nods.

Westlake High School, they agree, is a conservative place, both in its politics and its educational methods.

"When Zack was in my class at Westlake he was staring at the wall," says Kellie. Zack nods philosophically.

Back at Westlake, Kellie sensed, correctly, that Zack might have had the kind of suffocated intellect that surfaces to embrace debate as a cure for the banality of high school. Once she had him interested, she assigned him Foucault's *Discipline and Punish,* a seminal work of deconstructionist history that opens with descriptions of eighteenth-century torture. "He came back and told me, 'What have you done to me? I've done nothing for the past seventy-two hours but read this book.'"

This is a typical rebel-debater story, says Kellie. "A lot of debaters are smart—a lot of debaters have behavioral problems." She shrugs. When you watch the kids who are interested in debate file into the classroom, she says, "all of them are incredibly weird."

When Kellie—herself an avid debater and grade-grubber back at middle-class high schools near Houston and Austin—met Zack and Jack, she found herself much taken with "a couple of kids who went to a really rich school but didn't fit in there."

Jack, who is thin with wire-rimmed glasses, a turned-up nose, and long, straight blond hair, talks on one hand about being a musician—he plays drums in a band—and on the other about becoming a teacher or a civil rights lawyer. Jack is getting to be just as able at deploying the Continental postmodernists as Zack, and has asked his father not to put his debate trophies on the mantel because from an environmentalist perspective trophies waste materials, and because the point of debate is to say what you believe, not to win.

In fact, Zack and Jack have both come to reject the conventional success ethos on all fronts, and this has always presented a dilemma for Kellie. "Zack is off-the-charts smart, but his grades in school were bad because he doesn't care about school; he cares about debate. The situation you're faced with in high school is, 'I could either conjugate these bullshit Spanish words or I could read another hundred and fifty pages of Deleuze.' And we teach them to question the system, and then they challenge it. They argue that high school is detainment without probable cause, and they're kind of wrong but they're also kind of right."

Zack was ineligible to participate in debate for parts of his senior year because of his academic record. It was in spite of this, and in spite of a post-Kellie Westlake debate coach who didn't particularly care for national cross-x trips (thus prompting a Westlake debate-parents revolt) that Jack and Zack made it to Georgetown, where I met them. They'd paid for the flight themselves.

Written evidence of structured oral argument on a particular subject goes back at least as far as Plato's Socratic dialogues. Rabbinical debates about the Talmud and other Jewish religious texts go back thousands of years. In the United States, nineteenth-century debating societies inspired intercollegiate debate, and debate as it's practiced in American high schools and colleges remains a distinctly national tradition. The first known formal competition between two schools in American debate took place in Chicago in 1872, between the University of Chicago and Northwestern, and by 1892 Harvard was debating Yale. The National Forensics League, which organizes high-school and college debate at the national level, was founded at Ripon College in Wisconsin in 1931, and instituted a system of national tournaments. By midcentury, the majority of U.S. congressmen were graduates of high-school or college debate programs, although this figure has since waned. Today, debate still tends to attract extremely successful students; nearly 100 percent of high-school debaters go on to college. They are mostly middle- to upper-middle class; a 1990 study indicated that the majority came from families with yearly incomes over $45,000. The same survey found that of those who described their politics in terms of a party, 52 percent classified themselves as Republican and 26 percent as Democrat.[1]

For an entire tournament season, one topic is discussed at every serious policy debate competition. (This year it's whether the United States government should substantially increase funding for mandatory service programs for high-school students.) Shortly before a round of debate, one team is assigned with arguing this case in the affirmative (they are called "aff") while the other will argue this case in the negative. Because the affirmative team is allowed to go first and get in the last word, the negative team is permitted two turns in a row in the middle of the debate: the "negative block." The back-and-forth is structured like this: A-N-A-N-N-A-N-A. Within those bounds you can do pretty much whatever you want.

Because there are almost no actual rules at all, every once in a while somebody invents a new way to make an argument that

1. See Gary Alan Fine, *Gifted Tongues: High School Debate and Adolescent Culture.*

beats all the old ways, and changes the sport. In the late 1960s, at the college level, then the early 1970s, at the high-school level, the new weapon was speed. Speed transformed debate from a persuasion exercise into a strategy game, in which the object was to overwhelm your opponent with more arguments than they could possibly address. This is called "spreading the flow" or "spread and spew," the idea being that you are spreading your opponent thin. The result of all this is the gulps.

Who is to blame for this? Maybe Laurence Tribe, the big legal scholar. Tribe was part of a Harvard team that won the National Debate Tournament in 1961. (NDT is the single most important national tournament for college students.) In 1969 he coached a Harvard team to the same victory. In pictures of the event, Tribe stands between his wards wearing an opaque but friendly smile. Each of the wards, by contrast, has his jaw positioned in a way that says, "My mind is a dagger pressed against your throat."

"You'd best get the views of others on my role in this partly good and partly unfortunate development; I'm not sure my own recollections would be the most objective available," Tribe wrote me (this is how all lawyers talk to journalists). "For whatever those recollections are worth, my principal contribution, I think, was the whole idea of using flow charts on large (11" x 17" or larger) sheets of paper to follow the logical development of arguments in a debate; that I spoke very quickly while remaining comprehensible and trying to be persuasive was ancillary to that contribution. Many of the debaters who followed in my steps appear to have privileged speed and volume of coverage over subtlety and persuasiveness of content and even over comprehensibility by ordinary mortals."

Gradually, proponents of the new techniques became the most

influential judges, and the 1970s, '80s, and early '90s were the period in which Tribe's game-theory, computer-like, rational approach to debate was accepted as convention.

There were rebellions against spread and spew. The year 1979 saw the beginning of "Lincoln-Douglas," a new format that sought to provide an alternative to the speed and impenetrability of policy debate by giving points for language and presentation. But policy debate went and got its own avant-garde. It began to drift in a new direction: critical theory.

One person sometimes credited with introducing critical theory arguments into debate—these arguments are called "kritik" in debater parlance—is Brian McBride, now a debate coach at the University of Southern California. As an undergrad at the University of Texas in the early 1990s, he began to win debates by using postmodern philosophy to question the parameters of the argument, citing Foucault and other French philosophers popular in progressive English departments. The tactic broke into mainstream high-school debate usage in 1995, when, at the biggest national high-school debate tournament—the annual Tournament of Champions in Lexington, Kentucky—a team from Niles West High School in suburban Chicago, consisting of George Kouros and Armands Revelins, won using kritik. This was a watershed moment, and it didn't go smoothly or unnoticed.

"The level of theory was unusual simply because 'the kritik' was a pretty new argument in debate," says John Heintz, who coached Kouros and Revelins at Niles West. "My debaters said that the act of participating in a debate propagates discourse which creates reality . . . Some debaters wanted the judge to be a policymaker in Congress and vote for the 'best policy.' Other debaters wanted the judge to be an ethicist and make a moral choice . . . Rather, our debaters asked judges to think about the effect of the language chosen by the other team and vote against those choices. There was a lot of resistance. Some judges simply refused to evaluate them."

But even detractors from the kritik started to learn defenses against it, so today every national-grade debate camp teaches some critical theory. At the college level the form has broken wide open, begetting all manner of short-lived experiments.

"When I was in college there were literally people who would take all their clothes off and explain how that was an argument," Kellie recalls. "Or put tape over their mouths and then talk about feminism. I don't think reading a poem about the stars is a form of argumentation, but people can argue about *that*. It's the most laissez-faire system ever; if you're doing something that's bullshit, people will come up with good reasons why it's bullshit and it corrects itself."

As fun as all of that might be, debate is also something nerds do in order to meet other nerds they can hit on. The lobby of Georgetown Day Middle School during the Washington, DC, regional National Forensics League tournament is one of those ridiculously charged rooms full of adolescents learning to flirt. A pair of girls sit side-by-side, with one resting her legs upon the other's legs. A wavy-haired, rosy-cheeked boy from the Edgewood, New York, team addresses a slender, ponytailed girl who is locked in conversation with her friend. There is that almost-shouted mock hostility I remember from senior year of high school.

"Shut up!" the boy says, to cut through the noise in the room, and because he is young and witty, and wants the rest of us to be able to participate in the sparkling tableaux of which he and the girl will be the focal points.

"Shut *up*?"

"What's your record?"

She cocks her head to one side. "Two-two."

"Shut *up*."

There is no reason for his skepticism, but of course it is not really skepticism; it's an invitation to play. Boys and girls sit on arms of couches and read over one another's laptops. Forearms brush against shoulder blades, couches sag with the weight of many bodies, the spaces next to and between couches are covered with bodies sprawled, contorted, so that their owners can hear and participate in one or another group conversation. They are usually scattered across America, among so many nondebaters, and here they have entered an exclusive space where the codes they know are the codes that count, and they are in love with one another. The adults show deference; the middle-aged woman manning the table where refreshments are sold keeps her arms crossed on the table and her eyes on her copy of *Remembrance of Things Past*.

This is *Pride and Prejudice*. These are teenagers who've been provided with an adult-created community that comes with its own innocuous subject matter, and the innocuous subject matter works as an excuse for the all-important, tacitly adult-approved process of boys and girls learning to talk to one another. It's good to be Mary Bennet when the debate is going on, and you are reading at four hundred words per minute from the notes on the tub; between debates, it's good to be Elizabeth Bennet.

On August 17, 2007, a little over a year after I met him in Georgetown, Jack Jenkins, who drew the Gilles Deleuze tree on the easel, was in a car crash. Reports are still incomplete, but it seems in outline that he went to a party at Zack's new post-high-school apartment in Austin and offered to drive a drunk boy home in the drunk boy's car so he wouldn't get into an accident, and at reasonable speed hit a brick wall, sustaining injuries from the steering wheel to his chest and heart that killed him immediately. He was seventeen. The other boy walked away with a cut on his leg.

The other debaters from Westlake High, and some from the surrounding area, spent most of the next ninety-six hours together. "They spent the first twenty hours talking about real emotional issues, and I've never seen adults do this during grief," remembers Kellie. "And I think that comes from doing debate."

As I write, the debate team at Westlake High is planning a plaque that will feature a photograph of Jack carrying a box full of files and wearing a tie, ready for a debate round. It will run a Jack quote, maybe "It's chill," the reminder he'd always issue when someone was taking winning too seriously, but probably something else.

Jack's parents held a small memorial service at Rock Island, a monumental limestone formation in the flat center of Austin's Zilker Park, where Jack would go every weekend to meditate. Their speeches were filled with references to Nietzsche, and the evocation of the bard of individualism does seem appropriate for what Jack did, in choosing to throw over the academic path a smart kid is supposed to take for the thing he loved. He did what he thought it was his purpose in life to do, and given how little time on earth he was allotted it's hard to dispute that he did the right thing.

I talked to Jack's parents, Sarah and Scott Jenkins, on the phone, a month after the accident. Scott was a debater himself, he told me, in his San Antonio high school. (Sarah merely dated a debater.) Scott's debate partner for a year—this is back in the early 1970s—

was a boy named Dan. They lost touch soon after and never resumed contact. But after the private memorial service in Zilker Park there was an open reception with hundreds of guests in the Umlauf Sculpture Garden in Austin, and Scott was surprised to see a vaguely familiar face. Dan had heard about what happened. It had been more than thirty years, and his former debate partner had driven in from about a hundred miles away.

# case study:
# darren from the ghetto of amherst

Jack Jenkins and Zack Malitz found in their debate community a way to rebel against what they considered an overly regimented high-school existence. Their nerdy activity was a way out of a cage of false certainties.

Then there are other nerds for whom order is not a cage but a bright, clean Radisson in the snake-infested wilderness that is their daily life. For them, being a nerd is not a flight from an overly ordered existence; it's a flight from a life of fear and confusion into order. My friend Darren was such a nerd.

In ninth grade, we convened around an oak table every Tuesday after school on the second floor of the Jones Library, in a room intended for staff meetings. A librarian would poke her head in periodically to reassure herself it was the well-behaved, unattractive boys again, and she allowed us to spread ourselves, and our loose sheets of notebook paper with half-clothed ax-bearing women drawn on them, and our green, translucent dice, carried in little synthetic-cloth drawstring sacks, from wall to wall. The Dungeon Master was usually Darren, because of his charisma and air of impartiality and because it felt good—spiritually fulfilling, as a parent might phrase it—to follow a Dungeon Master who was black. Reality was not discussed, so we knew almost nothing about Darren's life.

Darren was light-skinned and tall with a hedge of black hair that gradually matured into an Afro. To the intense interest of the Jones Library D&D players, he seemed to have only white friends. His long hair, the pride and joy of the oak table because it was a monument to his blackness, was an affront to what Darren has since mournfully referred to as "the tiny clique of unassimilated black kids at our school." But the main problem, so far as said black kids were concerned, appeared to be that he hung out with us. They wouldn't leave him alone; I remember the way he would turn around and shrug as they would follow him through a hallway, calling him Mr. Wannabe White Guy.

We had a vague idea that he had been adopted by Seth's mom and had lived with Seth for two years in his loft bedroom, which looked like it was designed for snowshoe storage. We knew that since then he'd moved back in with his own mysterious mother, after a stretch of being adopted by the family of Eric Bernstein, whom our parents described as A Little Odd Maybe, it being 1991 and Asperger's syndrome not yet even a term that guidance counselors knew. We merely noted that Eric wore Rush T-shirts involving dragons, burped openly in class while teachers were speaking—without meaning to be the disrespectful burping student—and referred to himself as "frustrated" and "needing to take out his anger on something immediately." A good guy, and dedicated to the craft of boffing, certainly, but as a roommate, not ideal.

Darren's mother came to Massachusetts from England at sixteen. His father was a black American, a devout Christian, and a drinker who didn't realize he was one, "didn't know he was lost," as Darren puts it now. The Department of Social Services began to involve itself with the family of five—Darren had two younger brothers—when Darren was in third grade. They lived in an area known then and now as the Ghetto of Amherst.

In the Ghetto of Amherst there were/are homeless people who ask for money and rides in the parking lots, and tenants who smoke pot in the hallways, and tenants who leave their laundry hanging in the laundry room for days at a time because they are reluctant to pay the $1.50 a load and the dryers are frequently all occupied or broken. The ceilings leak, the cabinets do not reliably close, and the only chain that reliably delivers is Domino's; the rest often avoid the area due to safety concerns. Children run down the hallways and stairways making noise, maintenance does not eagerly respond to complaints, and the walls are thin.

Darren's mother was a heroin addict whose habit became debilitating around the time he was twelve. Today the smell of pot is a trigger that snaps Darren back to childhood, like the smell of chalk or the sensation of being grabbed by the upper arm. For him it was the regular stimuli of the apartment that also included P-Funk and corn bread. It was a black household, and Darren was a black kid, a mixed, light-skinned kid from East Hadley Road, with the raggedness of young children of real hippies.

This background—the Ghetto of Amherst, parents whose moods were linked to the availability of substances—did not prevent Darren from being nerdy. Rather, this background compelled Darren to seek out nerdiness.

Fourteen years later, I ask Darren why he went to the Jones Library to play Dungeons & Dragons after school. "We had each other in a very Stephen King sort of way; we didn't really have other people," he says.

In Stephen King's novel *It,* and his story "The Body," the basis for the movie *Stand By Me,* kids from small towns band together to confront horrors: shape-shifting killers, corpses, unhinged parents.

"You can tell," he says, "that those books are really about abuse, and about pain, and not being in control."

In sixth grade, things had deteriorated to the point where Darren's mother took out a restraining order against his father. His father came to Seth's birthday party out in Pelham, and tried to take away Darren's two little brothers. Darren helped pull them out of his father's car. His mother was in iffy physical condition by then, and Seth's mother, Allison, locally known as a feminist activist and artist, intervened by keeping Darren and his little brothers at her house. When I first met Darren, Seth's house was where he lived.

Seth's house had a combined living room and kitchen on the ground floor in which there were paths cut through hills of equipment and furniture, and a homemade stairway that led up into the darkness and heat of the low-ceilinged loft where Darren and Seth slept and played their Paleolithic salvaged Atari 2600. In the living room there were supplies for cooking and painting, mixed and sprinkled liberally over the nonmatching furniture, all of it tending to pile higher and higher toward a wall upon which a large framed canvas depicted a pile of naked female angels with thick pubic hair, reaching heavenward, perturbed but gallant, some embracing, some talking, some with small breasts and some with big ones. Their upwardly straining bodies formed a mountain so much like the living room's mounds of objects as to raise the possibility that the painting's truest subject was not the angels but the room in which it hung. There were tires in the yard, which became strategic obstacles in the games we played, cairns, dead land mines. It was a yard inhospitable to tag football but in its ruination suited to our purpose.

We made guns out of sticks and divided into two teams and huddled behind the gravel piles in the immense industrial gravel pit that lay beyond the limits of Allison's property, too old to be doing it, in love with the game and with the desert cleanliness of the landscape, of the civility of accepting that we had been shot and gamely falling sideways into the tiny gray rocks. Allison and her friends talked on picnic tables nearby.

Today, I ask Darren if he's still in touch with Seth. He shakes his head. "Our families don't get along." He lowers his eyes in an abstracted way. "I don't like airing other people's dirty laundry, but Allison was a nutter, albeit well-intentioned, and my brothers suffered the consequences, growing up there."

There were long sessions in which several of us would tuck ourselves into the sideways crevasse that was the loft, playing Defender and Jungle Hunt. In the Atari's chunky graphics, there was a clearness, a neatness, a starkness of contrast reminiscent of the gravel landscape in back of the house. The world was reduced to a black background interrupted by red stalagmites and vines, and a single figure rushing straight ahead to dispatch evil creatures. The spaceship or explorer traveled to the right while aliens and cannibals contrived to slow his progress. Nothing was cluttered—not nature, not outer space. Certainly virtue and sickness were not crowded into the same being.

In eighth grade, Darren moved back in with his mother, who was trying to clean up. ("Junkies are always trying to clean up," he said.) The gang from the oak table at the Jones Library celebrated his birthday at her little tan-carpeted living room/kitchen area, and I gave Darren a cassette of Sgt. Pepper's Lonely Hearts Club Band, which played on the stereo while he led us through a D&D adventure. His mother looked like an ethnicity I had never seen before, gaunt with brown hair pulled back in a tight ponytail, skin faintly yellow. I didn't know anything about her condition. A popcorn popper with a translucent yellow mouth was sitting in the sink and a bowl of popcorn was on the table.

"Where's the popper, Darren?" she demanded.

"In the sink, Ma," he said.

"Why'd you put it there?" Her voice rose to what sounded like its straining point, not very loud. "You're such an idiot." Darren looked at her for a moment, and she folded her arms, and stared down at the sink, and was silent for a while. The chain of imaginary skirmishes Darren had arranged rolled over his mother's silence, and she remained distant, insofar as the apartment would allow, lingering by the dishes and the fridge, away from the table and our embarrassed laughter.

"Here was ours," Darren remembers now, taking in the cobblestone plaza. By "ours" he means the freaks and geeks of our high school. There was the stoop of the Unitarian church, where the smokers would hunch. There was the grass in front of the Catholic church, opposite, where the faded-black-cotton/leather girls would sprawl. We both dated girls, sort of, without knowing whether we were really dating. One of them, who used to show me how to shoplift from CVS, stole his leather-backed copy of the first issue of Neil Gaiman's *The Sandman*. She also painted his thumb to show he was taken, the commitment ritual of the faded-black-cotton/leather girls. It was a new feeling, being a painted-thumb-level boyfriend, of being wanted sufficiently that measures were taken to prevent your running away.

Nobody in our group of friends knew it at the time, of course, but Darren's mother had AIDS and hepatitis C. While she was on one of her prolonged periods of kicking, when Darren was in college, she had a stroke. Her recovery did not go well, and he checked her into a retirement home where she died soon afterward. Six months later he wed; he's been married seven years now. He holds a BA in Japanese from the University of Massachusetts and works as an aide in a home for mentally retarded adults. His daughter is six.

I ask him what kept him so cool-headed during the years of our acquaintance, the evident leader of our group.

"I was good at faking it," he says. "I assumed you realized I was extremely angry."

I hadn't. Compared to the rest of us, he was a boy of steel. He never burst into tears when kids trailed him in the halls and yelled at him, never sulked off the field of battle when he lost all his limbs and was left just kneeling there. Once, in ninth grade, he and a kid named Orion decided to have a fight just to have a fight. They climbed to the top of a hill and began to hit each other, and neither backed down or ran away; they were dragged to the principal's office, where they were questioned thoroughly, and were not believed.

The reason he was able to keep up the iron-boy act was that gaming functioned for him then in some of the ways religion functions for him now.

When I meet Darren in downtown Amherst, he is taking his lunch break from a volunteer administrative shift at the Episcopalian church by the common. The link between the two practices—gaming and religion—was a feeling of being on a path, of pilgrim's progress. "I really remember knowing what would come next when you would level up and that was really comforting. It was rules and some measure of competency. Because we were incompetent to change our home lives, which were totally beyond our control."

The most famous nerds in pop culture—the nerds in *Revenge of the Nerds* and *Saturday Night Live,* say—come from boring, pleasant, homes. Their parents—Mr. Skolnick, Mrs. Loopner—are, like them, nice and nerdy, which indicates that childhoods have been on the structured, predictable side. (Mr. Skolnick has a laugh just like Louis's, and is gentle and friendly. Mrs. Loopner is just as gentle, and helpless in the realm of social interaction, as is her daughter.) Their nerdiness flows from their family lives. Darren's nerdiness was a bulwark against it.

# the cool nerd:
## superficial reflections on the hipster

I went to high school in the 1990s; my peers were the first generation of children raised by bourgeois bohemians.[1] Our parents
lived by the principle that you could walk with one arm around
the shoulder of the avant-garde and another around the shoulder
of the establishment, drunk on art *and* money. You could practice
law or run a foundation and still exercise the creative impulse
in the placement of your rock garden or in letters to the editor or
the Talking Heads song you played at your second wedding in a
renovated industrial structure. I remember watching, at sixteen,
my father get remarried, after weeks of macrobiotic dieting, in the
Manhattan offices of the foundation where he worked. I was
assigned to playing songs on a digital keyboard while people
mingled at the reception, and we'd settled the repertoire carefully.

1. See David Brooks, *Bobos in Paradise* for the origin of the term.

"Do *not* play 'Come on Baby, Light My Fire,'" my father calmly instructed. "Do *not* play 'Come on Baby, Light My Fire.'"

As I sat there playing "Love Me Two Times," I watched one of the dudes from Girls Against Boys, a band whose bass player is now a book editor, file in with one of my father's co-workers; I recognized him from a poster my friend had on the wall of his boarding-school dorm room. After the ceremony, everybody danced to a program of music distinguished by its hybridity, its mix of jazz, rock, jazz-rock, dance, and dance-rock, black music and white music. Being sixteen, I thought to myself: How do I rebel against this? How does my generation do something new? How do we construe this epoch as a rotting husk adrift on dark waters, so that we can make our own creative endeavors seem romantic?

One answer is purism. When eclecticism is your parents' thing you revisit old genres and deliberately maintain their integrity (these genres may have once themselves been considered hybrids, but a really long time ago). *Freak folk* is the rock-criticism name for my generation's exploration of folk music. *New garage* means my generation's take on mid-1960s guitar rock. *Nu wave* means my generation's take on early punk and new wave. In these albums, there is no hip-hop or jazz or Texas swing or house or any of the other flavors previous generations loved to mix. The sort-of-true clichés about what hipsters like—trucker caps, mustaches, Pabst Blue Ribbon, mullets—play with the idea of *old school*. They connote sophistication and cosmopolitanism by screaming, "We are not cosmopolitan! We are not culturally sophisticated!" This is an anti-Bobo trend, and one aspect of it is the flowering of nerdiness as an aesthetic.

To understand how the nerdiness aesthetic works, let's go way back to 1950s Norman Mailer. In 1957, Norman Mailer wrote an essay called "The White Negro: Superficial Reflections on the Hipster." His argument was that rebellious white people were learning from an oppressed, constantly endangered sector of the population— black people—how to behave in a time of conformity and fear of the atom bomb, in the wake of a war that proved the inhumanity of governments. "The Negro (all exceptions admitted) could rarely afford the sophisticated inhibitions of civilization," he wrote, "and so he kept for his survival the art of the primitive, he lived in the enormous present, he subsisted for his Saturday night kicks, relinquishing the pleasures of the mind for the pleasures of the body." The Negro, in other words, was used to living under threat (Mailer believed), and so by adopting his mentality white hipsters could find a way to preserve that which was precious in their souls during the atomic age.

What we have right now, in Brooklyn, the Bay Area, Portland, East Los Angeles—neighborhoods where bourgeois young people work at magazines, movie studios, TV shows, Web sites and advertising, so that cultural trends work like weather at sea, offering the newcomers a chance to prove themselves, upending the complacent—is a similar choice on the part of the privileged to identify with the outsider. The outsider in this case is the nerd, because nerds are people incapable of, or at least averse to, riding cultural trends. When your greatest fear is that you will become a loser because your intuition will fail to keep up with tastes, you embrace the nerd like a little harmless teddy bear who's the one creature in the whole wide world who would never do anything to hurt you.

This doesn't mean that being a nerd is like being black, let alone being black in the 1950s. (Mailer's account of being black in the 1950s is maybe sketchy anyway.) It means that nerds are a group by definition incapable of riding trends the ways that people in the creative professions need to ride trends. Nerds are the outsiders that hipsters gesture toward as a way of signaling an awareness and rejection of those forces that shape their lives.

The fake nerd, like the white Negro, is a way of dealing with constant threat. The threat, in this case, is a lot milder than that of nuclear war, but it's the single largest threat that hangs over the lives of creative professionals in major cities: losing momentum in your career, losing the aura of an up-and-comer, acquiring the odor of failure. In practical terms, losing your job or losing some or all of your freelance jobs, acquiring a reputation for "struggling" that turns into pariah status (one of the worst features of life in the creative professions is that one professional mishap or gap between jobs can make you a perceived failure and this scent can repel potential employers and render you an actual, quantifiable failure). The nature of work in the media, broadly defined, is that it's insecure and transient. Survival depends on maintaining a register of acquaintances who think you're good at what you do, think you're cool, want to hire you, have the power to do so, and haven't been rejected by you sexually. There's often careerist hustle in the depths of friendships, even when the surface is calm. Nerds, by contrast, go through life getting advanced degrees and being recruited and applying for things, learning rules from textbooks. Sometimes, to the media/entertainment industry's young, sensitive, subproletariat, that sounds like Shangri-La. On the streets of major cities and college towns, you see the bulky glasses, the cardigans, the high pants, the Loopnerish plastic barrettes. These are tributes to nerdiness.

There is a new version of Richard Yates's immortal couple in *Revolutionary Road,* the Wheelers. They live in Park Slope, or Silver

Lake, or Wicker Park. "God," they sometimes think, "in a way, wouldn't it be kind of nice to be an engineer in the fifties? Not really with all that sexism and conformity and *general attitude of fascism,* you know? And discomfort about sexuality? But just not *trying* to be someone you're *not?*"

I took my first stab at being a fake nerd when I was seventeen, roughly three years after I initiated my effort not to be a real nerd. I bought a pair of black Elvis Costello/Malcolm X glasses. I cut my hair from a bass-player volcano to a midlength floppy mushroom shape. I was supposed to be an attractive parody of my old self. For being a fake nerd, like being a white Negro, can be a way of putting even more distance between yourself and the object of your imitation than there was before. In the imagination of the fake nerd, the nerd is attractive because he is unaffected, untrendy to the point of primitivism, a kind of inert noble savage. Going through life making the exertion of affecting noble savagery makes you feel even less a noble savage than you did before. Being a fake nerd leaves you less of a nerd. Which is why it's an excellent strategy for former nerds. You can both acknowledge your past (obeying the teenage principle of don't-reinvent-yourself-or-we'll-call-you-a-poser) and distance yourself from it (I am so indisputably un-nerdy I can wear accessories and even pants that are nerdy and not be a nerd). This is why when you go to a party full of young music studio engineers, or arts journalists, or book editors, you look around and see a fake nerd uniform (bulky glasses, floppy hair, sweaters, low-top canvas sneakers useless for athletic activity).

You hear fake nerd conversation. It follows a model. You bring up an "obsession" or "total fascination" with a purportedly unfashionable subject. "I am such a dork about old Hawaiian slide guitar. I actually have every King Benny record. I've so got a problem."

"Dude, you want to hit In-N-Out burger? I basically live on their Protein Burgers when I'm in LA."

This is a way of whipping out cultural capital, but not in the same way as leaving guests in the living room to retrieve a hollow-body guitar or a first edition of *To The Lighthouse*. The Gretsch and the Woolf say, "I am creative and educated, so I have an understanding of the blues and the Bloomsbury Group." The Hawaiian slide recordings and the In-N-Out Burger, which are both low-end consumer products, say, "I love the things I love because I am guided by some untamed voice within me that causes me to have random obsessions. I will follow my individualized obsessions, not trends, and be transparent about those obsessions, even when those obsessions tell me to like things widely considered ugly and cheap." It's the cultural capital of quirk.

To receive transmissions from God, the people doing the Quirky Nerd thing cultivate hair that reaches for the heavens. The hair is the hair of Booger, the violinist in *Revenge of the Nerds,* of Albert Einstein, of Napoleon Dynamite. There's no appreciable cult of Booger, but pictures of Einstein with his hair in bloom, his eyes serene, hang in offices and teenage bedrooms, including those where physics are seldom discussed, as a watchful agent of God. Napoleon Dynamite has become part stuffed animal, part clown, part saint.

In *Napoleon Dynamite,* the saintly aspect of Napoleon's character comes from his inability to conform and the way that inability excites a rebellious spark in others. The climax takes place at an assembly at an Idaho high school, where the two candidates for class president compete for the affection of their peers and Napoleon performs a funk dance routine on behalf of his friend Pedro. Instead of booing, the crowd rises in a standing ovation and awards Pedro the election over the popular girl expected to win. It's not like the class has secretly admired Napoleon the whole time. It's that when the nerd goes over the top into super-nerdy he makes everyone want to be more authentic and less judgmental. That shoot-the-moon play for social acceptance is what informs the quirky-nerd look when performed by self-conscious young hipsters. You're a menace to social uniformity, in some unspecified fashion, through your natural and heedless iconoclasm.

It's also just barely possible to think you make a statement about gender when you work a fake nerd look. While nerds, as everybody knows, tend to be male more often than female, dressing like a nerd rejects conventional ideas about what a hunky young man looks like. Since conventional notions of what makes a young man look handsome are so bound up with conveying power and wealth and the capacity for punching somebody out, making yourself look like a nerd on purpose is a gesture that says, "I renounce the privilege of being a young swinging dick." At the very least, it's a refusal to make your outfit a monument to your own authority. For a woman, dressing up as fake nerd is a refusal of plumage. In an androgynous paradise where adults of both sexes look like enlarged spelling-bee champions, it's easy to forget for a moment, or even an entire night of drinking beer, that privilege is unevenly distributed between genders. At least, it's easy if you're male.

Being a fake nerd doesn't just offer a way to downplay gender privilege; it offers a way to downplay class privilege. Tom Wolfe wrote a piece for *Commentary* magazine in 1976 that described American politics as a high-school cafeteria writ large. He argued that people vote according to their high-school identity; jocks and cheerleaders vote conservative, hoods and nerds vote liberal. (This is not unlike Paul Feig's ruminations on the same subject.) When Americans vote for a particular candidate, they vote for the candidate who reminds them of the kind of person they would have eaten lunch with.

Fake nerds are acting out this lunchroom version of American politics. The overwhelmingly liberal artists, grad students, editors, and so on who practice fake nerdiness are taking an identity that people are assigned as children and choosing it as an identity in adulthood. Whereas people used to dress in such a way that showed they belonged to a particular socioeconomic class, fake nerds dress in such a way that refers to a bygone phase of life when they didn't occupy any particular place as workers in the economy, when they were members of separate but not necessarily always equal tables in high school.

Looking out over a party on the Lower East Side thrown by a journalist and a editor, I saw a crowd of people dressed as if the creative industries were a high-school clique: nerds. All of the symptoms rarely manifested themselves in one person, but about half the guests displayed at least one nerd accessory (big glasses, short pants, hand-me-down rugby shirt). To look at this party, you'd think fake nerd was the uniform of the cash-poor upper middle class.

Has the fake-nerd uniform replaced the hippie one? Is fake nerdiness countercultural? Sort of. Among the boomers' kids, and the middle-aged punk-rock generation that came of age in the late 1970s and 1980s, there's an established skepticism toward the idea that the most important thing about the 1960s counterculture was that it was an authentic, anticommercial, anticorporate flowering of rebellious spirit. In 1997, Thomas Frank's book *The Conquest of Cool* argued that the victories of the counterculture took place in the realm of pop culture—in chart-topping albums like *Beggars Banquet,* in hit movies like *Bonnie and Clyde*—and were partly the results of marketing, radio promotion, and publicity campaigns. As Frank remarked, what was so interesting about the late 1960s was the way that corporate executives embraced the freaks. The movies sympathetic to the counterculture that came out in the late 1960s and early 1970s (*Easy Rider, Shampoo*) showed young hippies and outlaws losing their struggles against the iron heel of conservative America (the heel was made of rednecks with shotguns, police, and Republican financiers). But in retrospect the story of the sixties counterculture looks not so much like a battle with business culture as a joint effort to reshape the status quo. Advertisers designed trippy green ads for 7UP. *Time* ran trippy covers featuring Swinging London and eventually The Band.

If this is your story of the late 1960s, there's something faintly ridiculous, or at least insufficiently self-aware, about dressing like a hippie to be rebellious. Being a hippie is outdoorsy, left-of-center, chill, but not subversive. The most enthusiastic proponents of the sixties counterculture in the 1990s rural Massachusetts of my youth were the boarding-school kids who went to Phish shows. It was a good-natured acknowledgment of privilege to go on the jam-band circuit, a preppy thing. Hippies were politically conscientious but inoffensive, too derivative to make anybody nervous.

Dressing like a punk was not a solution. Everyone knew that aesthetic was helping to move twenty-dollar Warped Tour tickets. There was no reason to even consider hip-hop; nobody who lived in a city with cable television and billboards could doubt *that* was a movement working in collusion with business culture to sell suburban teenagers stuff, even if was admirably forthright of rappers to dress like gay Moët Hennessy-Louis Vuitton executives and sing about how purely commercial their motives were. Of course in all of these movements, hip-hop included, there were artists in garrets, making music for the music, but nobody wanted to run the risk of being mistaken for one of the kids who fell for the marketing.

With the biggest subcultures built around a style of music and comportment out of commission, there was still an identity left to try on. We know which lunch table we're circling now. If you want to become an adult member of the chattering classes, the words "I'm *such* a punk," or "I'm *such* a hippie" refuses to roll off your tongue. "I'm *such* a nerd" comes more naturally. The nerd receives his calling from God or nature, not from television and magazines, even if that calling is playing video games or programming computers. The nerd can't sell out because the nerd is incapable of selling out.

Soon, this tactic will be obsolete. The Tripwire, a music-focused trend-reporting service affiliated with *Fader* magazine, has a piece today about an English clothing company that incorporates images from Atari 2600 games into the patterns on its polo shirts. There's a *Geek* magazine, and there are "I Love Nerds" shirts with the letters designed to look like homemade iron-ons. Self-styled "nerdcore" rappers wear pocket protectors and rhyme about hard drives. As I write this, CBS is working on a new fall sitcom called *The Big Bang Theory,* in which two nerds try to win the heart of one pretty woman, even though its corporate partner, the CW network, will be airing a new season of its hit reality show *Beauty and the Geek,* in which eight nerds try to win the hearts of eight pretty women. Last spring, the CW's president of entertainment, Dawn Ostroff, offered a simple justification for this seemingly inexcusable, unsynergistic, nerd/hottie courtship programming glut: "Nerds are really in right now."

Advertisers and writers alike have been selling America on the uncool outsider for a long time. At first the call was to be nonconformist. The 1950s were the decade when "conformity" became a frequently discussed social ill, but Sinclair Lewis wrote *Babbitt*, a novel in which the "standardization" of American suburban life is the chief subject, during the early 1920s, not long after America first emerged as one of the most powerful and economically healthy countries in the world. Then the appeal to consumers to not conform by trying too hard to be nonconformist cropped up in advertising in the 1960s, when a magazine ad for Volvo (of course) depicted an enemy Ford dealership plastered with slogans proclaiming Ford "The New Fun Look of Youth." Volvo's copy read, "Your car is out of style. Again. And the irony of it is, a big chunk of the money that you paid for your out-of-style car was used to bring out the very cars that put it out of style."[2] The supposed appeal of the Volvo was the appeal of the nerd: I'm cool because I don't waste effort on being cool; I have too much substance for that. But of course if that strategy becomes overly familiar, practiced by a critical mass of trendy individuals and advertisers, it becomes suspect.

Let the publication of these words then herald the death of nerd chic. People will find another class of person supposedly incapable of fashionable affectation. Soon there will be a trend piece, in some respectable publication somewhere, called "Revenge of the Jocks."

2. Thomas Frank, *The Conquest of Cool*.

# nerd love

## two utopias

Live the Dream holds its meetings in a polymarriage house here in Winnetka, half an hour from LA, in an inconspicuous white one-and-a-half-story house. This is the home of Terry, Paul, Marcus, Laura, Carl, and Will. Inside the living room, a tall, realistic painting of Adam and Eve, the tree, the fruit, and the serpent hangs over the television, which shows *The Passion of Ayn Rand*. Terry and Paul stop to kiss more than anyone else, but there is foot-touching going on all around.

Live the Dream is a small organization consisting largely, I suspect, of the residents of this house. Its purpose it to spread the practice of polymarriage. Meetings are open to the public and take place the third Saturday of every month. At this one, first five, then all six of the residents are engaged in a conversation with the film, advertised in the Live the Dream newsletter as concerning Ayn Rand's "poly relationship with Nathaniel Branden." (Branden was Rand's prodigy.) Rand's inner circle is Olympian-level hot. When Nathaniel Branden's wife, played by Julie Delpy, becomes jealous of his woman on the side, Paul, who is wearing a plaid shirt and large metallic glasses, says "Wrong!"

"Yeah, what is that?" says Terry.

Carl makes the game-show wrong-answer buzzer noise.

"That's not the poly way of handling it," says Terry. "Bring her into the relationship too—that's the poly way."

"That's right," says Paul.

Of Nathaniel Branden, played by Eric Stoltz, Terry says, "I went to see him once. He was really good."

"Were you inexplicably drawn to him?" asks Paul.

"No," says Terry. "But I am inexplicably drawn to you." They move in for a long kiss. Later on, Ayn Rand cusses out Nathaniel Branden for cheating on his wife and thus threatening the unity of the inner circle of Objectivism; Helen Mirren slaps Eric Stoltz in the face.

"That's emotionalism!" says Carl. "She wouldn't have believed in that."

This is how physical affection flows on the perpendicular couches: Paul and Terry cuddle, Terry's right foot is stretched out slightly in the direction of Carl, who rests the toes of his own left foot on top of that right foot. To Carl's right, Laura and a man with long hair and glasses, Marcus, are cuddling. Will joins us close to the end and sits between Laura and Carl, touching no one.

"I was really interested in the idea that you guys developed a lifestyle on the teachings of a book," I say.

"But that's not so unusual," says Carl. "I mean that's what Ayn Rand did—she wanted her book to teach people how to live a certain way, just like the Bible."

The discussion turns to the Church of All Worlds, founded in the 1960s and based on a church of the same name in the Heinlein novel *Stranger in a Strange Land*. What captivates me as I sit across from the members of the group household (nobody else is here at this point in the special event but me and the residents of the house) is the faith in reading. *A recent novel contains a model for living; we will execute it without emotionalism because, as it says in the Live the Dream newsletter, "This kind of marriage best preserves assets, takes care of kids, and creates FAMILY," and then we'll invite the public to come see.* The chain of middle-aged hands and feet, spread over the two couches, is not sensual so much as pious. These are people who have woven their sexuality into what they consider to be a moral way of living they have learned from wise texts; if the outside world considers it deviant, it doesn't matter. If this is sexual deviance, it's sexual deviance as part of a plan that includes children, household expenses, and everyday life. Courting and romance are usually governed by a mix of convention and what Carl might call emotionalism. But Live the Dream has found a way to make it appear, at least, to be governed by reason.

On the other hand, nerds who harbor the great *otaku* obsessions—anime, comic books, and their related gaming spin-offs—sometimes embrace a sexuality built to accommodate a bubble of eternal childhood. Witness the opening ceremony at the Third Annual Anime Los Angeles Convention. The conference room is full of teenagers who are being addressed by a middle-aged man with a beard and a Hawaiian-style black-and-yellow shirt with Asian letters in lieu of tropical flowers. He has translucent brown nerd glasses, and he wears a pair of furry bear ears on top of his head.

"Chaz it up! Chaz it up!" shout the teenagers, in a ritualistic way, because this man, whose name is Chaz Boston Baden, is chairman of Anime Los Angeles. To his right sit two female manga artists, creators of the comics "Dramacon" and "OniKimono," and at the other end of the lineup sits another middle-aged male MC, Tadao Tomomatsu, who throws candy and individually packaged marshmallows into the crowd.

Chaz runs down the activities on the schedule, pausing to explain the Mad Gothic Tea Party.

"This is an experiment: I didn't want to come out and say, 'Elegant Gothic Lolita Day,' because parents don't always understand what that means . . . But I want to see you all in your *Alice in Wonderland* dresses."

Anime Los Angeles 3 is more *otaku* than straight-up nerd; there isn't a single computer, knight, or spaceship in sight. The crowd contains a real-life soldier from Camp Pendleton, seated next to me, wearing his full army greens, backpack, and camouflage headkerchief; a girl with a blue hairdo culminating in two symmetrical puffs, a black shirt with puffy sleeves, and a puffy, bell-shaped bottom half; a girl with a backpack in the shape of a Pokémon creature; a chubby teenage boy with no shirt, red pants tucked into boots, eye patch, goatee, wristband. (The hobby of dressing up like a manga character is called CosPlay.) They're most excited to hear from the author of *Dramacon,* Svetlana Chmakova, who is being interviewed by Chaz.

The pitch of Chaz's voice becomes slightly higher.

"What kind of chocolate do you like? Nuts and chews? Or soft centers?"

The chocolate inquiry lasts for roughly five minutes, longer than the story of Svetlana's immigration from Russia and discovery of manga. The teenagers call out from the crowd:

"Chewy!"

"Soft center!"

Tomomatsu: "I'm a softy!"

Audience: "Awwwww!"

*Lolita, Alice in Wonderland,* Pokémon, chocolate, candy, marshmallows, puns, soft swords, costumes, huge manga eyes, huge manga smiles, "awww." The common denominator at Anime Los Angeles 3 isn't Japan; it's childhood. With the masquerades (there are three) and the attention to dress and makeup and hair, these young people, for whom pubescence is relatively new, and this middle-aged man overseeing them are using childishness as a tool for mild flirtation and group uplift. The single most frequent sight at the convention is the mutual fussing over and photographing of costumes; flirting in a context of Never Never Land, of sugar and euphoria.

The next day, Chaz and his wife stand in line for sandwiches at the hotel coffee shop. A girl who looks about seventeen, beautiful face, spiky hair, Sgt. Pepper's costume, cut off at a diagonal across her body to reveal stockings, approaches Chaz, who is still wearing the furry ears.

"Do you have a tattoo?" she asks Chaz.

"I don't have a tattoo," he responds, in measured tones, without a hint of salaciousness. "And my daughter's not here, so . . ."

The girl thanks him and leaves.

As Chaz and his wife walk down the hall, another teenage girl approaches Chaz with a little journalist's notebook and asks him what foods he likes to eat.

Time for the improv group. The Whose Line Is It Animé troupe will perform in a second conference room, and the seats are all full. War nymphs sit cross-legged on the carpet.

There are three men: one college-aged with long dark hair and long dark robes, one middle-aged with a red and black doublet, one twenty-something with a goatee; and a woman in blue and white sorceress robes with a wig of white fluff piled on top of her head. The format is called "If You Know What I Mean."

"Do you know where the *yaoi* panel is, if you know what I mean?" goatee asks dark robes. (*Yaoi* is manga that tells a gay love story.)

"I've got a *yaoi* panel right here, if you know what I mean," says dark robes.

Big laughs. Goatee grins and looks around.

A chant breaks out, the famous one from the 1932 film *Freaks:* "One of us! One of us! One of us!"


Becoming a different person and having sex or making out as that alternate person: this is a practice that exists in most nerd worlds. At one point, in Arizona, three knights in a tent strongly encouraged me and my friend Clay, who was filming everything for me, to prolong our stay. "You really have to stay for the night to get a sense of this place," one said. "Everybody starts drinking—you guys will get so laid." I saw a princess sit in a knight's lap. I saw a boy archer flirt with a girl archer, the two of them silhouetted with their bows and quivers against the desert sky like Tolkien elves. As dusk fell, more and more often I saw aristocrats of the opposite sex stand close to one another with beers, surprisingly like the cover of a romance novel, and really beautiful.

## the penis-for-mind trade

Sitting in his office at Rensselaer Polytechnic Institute, a couple of buildings away from the RPI *Bachelor* archives, Ron Eglash tells me a story about the divination priests of Senegal. "These guys did this amazing recursive mathematics, and they all had some kind of physical deformity," he explains.

"One of them pointed to his foot, which was sort of twisted off center. And he said, 'This is the price that I pay for my power.'" Eglash remembers what happened when he told the story at a lecture in Oregon. "A mathematician came up to me and he said, 'I was suddenly hit with this epiphany that I paid the same price but it's not physical deformity, it's social deformity; I'm a nerd.' It's much the same thing. You pay the price and you're given the power."

It might be overwrought to call that social deformity a castration, but it's a denial of sexuality. The rituals of masculine physicality that come with a more "normal" male adolescence and young adulthood are the ones nerds pretty much by definition forgo.

"When I was at UCLA," Eglash recalls, "I noticed all these fraternities would have all these beer busts and parties, high alcohol consumption—but it was all made as public as possible. All these things that could be going on inside the fraternity house are going on *outside* on the front lawn. It was a kind of desperate attempt to earn your stripes as a non-nerd, as a hard-partyer, with the thought

that when you take on Dad's business and become middle management you're going to need that experience to look back on. 'This is
Frank, but back when I knew him in college he was called Moon-
dog.'"[1]

The demasculinized image of the nerd, says Eglash, is cited by
social scientists as a reason certain socioeconomic groups don't
produce engineers in large numbers. This is the paradox, as Eglash
sees it, at the heart of the nerd's place in society. On the one hand,
the nerd is a despised figure, a failure of masculinity. On the other
hand, that very demasculinized image is associated with professions that wield economic power and the ability to transfigure
other people's lives. The fact that engineers historically tend to be
white and Asian males benefits white and Asian males, and not because the engineers are racists trying to uphold a Caucasian patri-
archy. "Voice recognition software works better on men's voices
because a bunch of engineers are sitting around in the lab and they
say, 'Charlie, come over here, I want to try your voice,'" Eglash explains. "Over time they build that social environment into the software. Camera film was created by these chemists and when they
wanted to try it out, they said, 'Hey Charlie, come over here,' and
Charlie's a white guy, and so in the end the cameras work better on
white people because you have all these white people trying it out

---

1. A character named Anthony Blanche, in *Brideshead Revisited,* says of the
   Oxford men who almost throw him in a fountain, "When they're all married to scraggy little women like hens and have cretinous, porcine sons
   like themselves, getting drunk at the same club dinner in the same
   coloured coats, they'll still say, when my name is mentioned, 'We put him
   in Mercury one night,' and their barn-yard daughters will snigger and
   think their father was quite a dog in his day, and what a pity he's grown so
   dull."

and fine-tuning it. Not because these guys are racist but because of the social environment in which it's getting created." In other words, the nerd image isn't a conspiracy to keep the sciences white and male in the interest of white men; it's a systemic tendency that helps keeps the sciences white and male and thereby inadvertently empowers white men.

## yaoi

While there are a lot of nerds who are exclusively into Hundred Years War–between-France-and-England-only-with-dragons novels, a lot of nerds like love stories. Duh; but it's worth noting that there are nerd subcultures (American manga comic-book fans, for instance) that have largely female sub-subcultures preoccupied with plugging different variables into particular romance narratives. In other words, there are a lot of nerds out there who read romance novels the same way people read Hundred Years War–between-France-and-England-only-with-dragons novels.

In the West, *yaoi* usually means a work of fiction involving a male-male romance in a style associated with Japanaese manga. The word is actually derived from the first syllables of the phrase, *yama noshi, ochi nashi, imi nashi,* which means "no peak, no point, no meaning," probably because the genre has been a staple of amateur manga and fan fiction. (An American analogy for this is a subgenre of *Star Trek* fan fiction called K-S, which consists mostly of love and sex between Captain Kirk and Spock.) The appeal of *yaoi* overlaps to a large degree with the appeal of *Brokeback Mountain*: two beautiful men get it on. The difference is that *yaoi* manga are comic-book stories about male homosexual love written by and for straight women.

Part of the standard formula is that one of the men/boys should be way manlier and less boyish than the other, so that one plays the role traditionally occupied by the pursued woman and the other that of the male suitor. One theory about the appeal of *yaoi* is that this structure allows women to identify with either or both conventional gender roles, whereas in a conventional heterosexual romance novel the woman (with whom female readers are supposed to identify) is usually the more passive party in the relationship. Female readers of *yaoi* manga are given the choice of craving the top boy or the bottom boy, thereby positioning themselves in the fantasy as dominant or submissive while remaining comfortably heterosexual.

But those female readers of *yaoi* also seem to love to plug different inputs into the same model to see what you get. The stories in *yaoi* are highly plot-driven and focus on how the circumstances that brought these two men together alternately cement and thwart their mutual attraction. In one *yaoi,* they're cops on a difficult murder case; in another they're firemen, and in another knights, and so on. Everyone knows they're going to hook up, that one will be the top and one will be the bottom. But there's still fun to plug different scenarios into the *yaoi* model to see what happens. Even in the nerd love story there's a little bit of computer-game playfulness.

# the autism spectrum

Wrong Planet, a Web site for people with Asperger's syndrome, houses a forum on the nature and utility of small talk. One tutorial goes like this:

> Alan: (originating) I played the course at Pebble Beach the other day.
> Beatrice: (receiving) What a nice day to do it.
> Beatrice: (originating) I went to the beach there a couple of years ago and thought it was gorgeous.
> Alan: (receiving) It's funny: I've been there several times, but I've never left the golf course!

And the conversation will continue in this vein until the two part and begin anew with other people. We Aspies would likely label this chit-chat as drivel, if we didn't know to look for the pattern underneath the superficial exchange.

This is the lesson that somebody in *Pride and Prejudice* needs to teach Mary Bennet, and that somebody in *Right Ho, Jeeves* needs to teach Gussie Fink-Nottle. Beneath the superficialities of small talk there is a give-and-take pattern that gradually bonds conversers to one another. There is no consistent set of codes, like those of the male newt, but there are vague rules that can be made intuitive and come to seem natural.

The urge to small talk is irrational, and when the ham-radio enthusiasts upbraided one another for "chin music" and womanly gabbing, they attacked that urge. The desire for rule-bound, rational communication is the desire that bonds so many groups we intuitively think of as nerdy: D&D players, computer programmers, ham-radio hobbyists, sci-fi fans. And it links them all to people on the autism spectrum.

The definition of Asperger's syndrome is a fraught one, but the general consensus is that "Aspies" have some of the qualities of autistics only without the low IQ and learning disabilities that characterize autism. The degree to which they have these qualities varies widely; some are borderline autistic, others don't appear to have a syndrome of any kind until you get to know them well. One scholarly article[1] on helping people with Asperger's learn communication skills described "those children or adults who need our intervention" this way:

1. "The Language of Social Communication: Running Pragmatics Groups in Schools and Clinical Settings," by Elsa Abele and Denise Grenier, from *Asperger's Syndrome: Intervening in Schools, Clinics, and Communities.* Full disclosure: this anthology was coedited by my mother, a psychologist whose area of specialty is Asperger's syndrome.

These individuals often and unintentionally behave in what others experience as an irritating manner. They consistently invade others' personal space, carry on about arcane topics, interrupt conversations, talk more loudly or softly than a situation dictates, or speak with an incorrect emphasis on words or word syllables in a sentence. Such a person might change the topic of conversation abruptly, or gaze in a different direction from the person to whom he or she is speaking, exhibiting poor eye contact. These are the children who have few or no friends or the adults we might tire of at a cocktail party.

These individuals would include an exceptionally large fraction of the souls at the Los Angeles Science Fantasy Society (and said souls know this about themselves). Asperger's syndrome is a neurological condition whose outward manifestations, at their mildest, sometimes resemble those of the social conditions we like to label, with unscientific abandon, as nerdy. Autism spectrum disorders have reasonably exact criteria for diagnosis; this is not the case with the folk diagnosis "nerd." But if you line up the traits of people and fictional characters who are nerds with the traits that comprise Asperger's, the overlap is hard to ignore. As noted before, Jerry Lewis's Kelp in *The Nutty Professor* is one of the most autism-spectrum characters Hollywood's created. In addition to his hyperliteral interpretation of questions, he has poor motor skills, another autism-spectrum issue, which causes him to break equipment at the gym; he even walks in a way that seem unsocialized, nonintuitive. He's a pop-culture illustration of a scientifically validated category.

The single most important aspect of the autism spectrum is an impairment of what psychologists call theory of mind. Theory of mind is the ability to attribute independent mental states to oneself and others in order to predict and explain behavior. The classic test of theory of mind in four-year-olds is called the Sally-Anne test, in which two dolls, Sally and Anne, sit facing each other, Sally with a box, Anne with a basket. A marble lies between them. Sally places the marble in the box. Anne then goes for a walk, leaving her basket. While she's gone, Sally takes the marble out of the box and puts it in the basket. Then Sally returns from her walk.

The tester asks the four-year-old, "Where will Sally look for the marble first?" Most four-year-olds figure out that Sally will look in the box first, but many autism-spectrum four-year-olds who have normal cognitive and language skills will not be able to solve the problem. People with Asperger's don't utterly lack theory of mind; they just find it more difficult to develop than neurologically typical ("NT" in "Aspie" slang) people do.

One symptom of the theory of mind issue is a failure to read social cues. A facial expression that others can read intuitively (or at least learn to read instantaneously) is often a puzzle to somebody with Asperger's, who may have to learn the language of tones and faces by rote. The ripples from this effect are the usual self-flagellation and anger that attend social disgrace.

"From my clinical experience," the Australian Asperger's scholar Tony Attwood has written, "a client with Asperger's syndrome is his or her own worst critic and is more likely to develop a social phobia due to self-criticism for making a social mistake." Not knowing what people are trying to communicate to you, and knowing that you don't know what people are trying to communicate to you: it's hard to think of more fertile ground for paranoia.

When I call Attwood, he becomes mildly inflammatory on the

subject of high-school social life: "The most rigid and intolerant group is teenagers—they are the most rule-bound group you can imagine and they have these thought-police that beat up anybody in the halls who's different from them." In other words, a group that understands a set of rules intuitively (how to be popular) abuses another group that comes to understand a different set of rules logically. Attwood has absolutely no problem with my elision of Asperger's syndrome with those traits and interests usually thought of as nerdy: people with Asperger's syndrome tend to be socially alienated and unusually focused on objects and systems, and while these are universal inclinations, it's "the degree" that distinguishes somebody with Asperger's from a neurotypical nerd.

One of the leading authorities on Asperger's is the Cambridge psychologist Simon Baron-Cohen, cousin of comedian Sacha "Borat" Baron Cohen. One of his contributions to the field was to describe Asperger's as "the extreme male brain," and both he and Attwood often point out that Asperger's is a disability only because it exists within a particular cultural context, that is, one in which everybody is expected to have particular social skills. Baron-Cohen found that a large percentage of people with Asperger's become engineers and scientists and that 15 percent of all Aspies have an engineer in their family—about three times higher than average.

The form of social awkwardness that Asperger's engenders is machinelike. Of course, this doesn't mean that people with Asperger's are subhuman or part machine, or actually like machines—it means that their social awkwardness is created by difficulty in reading the kind of human communication that machines also find difficult to read (facial expressions, eyes, tone of voice). Just as a computer can easily understand a set of verbal commands following a particular grammar, so can a person with severe Asperger's (or even autism). Their social awkwardness is reminiscent of, or evocative of, machines. Their impairment lies in the department of what is vernacularly called "animal instinct"—an intuitive, rather than logically derived, sense of what others are feeling and how to react.

So the overlap between nerdiness and Asperger's symptoms looks like this:

| NERDINESS | SHARED | ASPERGER'S |
|---|---|---|
| | Social phobias | |
| | Science, engineering | |
| | Rule-bound speech | |
| No physical confrontation | | |
| | Spastic movements | |
| | | Repetitive movements |
| | Intense focus on a particular subject or set of subjects | |

Asperger's syndrome occurs more often in regions where there are large numbers of computer programmers, which is to say regions where there are large numbers of nerds. Silicon Valley's unusually high rates of disorders on the autism spectrum are the most famous, but there are also off-the-charts numbers in the Route 128 tech company zone near Boston and the "Silicon Fen" area of England. Attwood told me that while he usually speaks to an audience the size of a normal classroom in a major city, when he speaks in Silicon Valley six hundred people show up. The same is true of Seattle and Houston—the tech hubs. This seems like a scientific validation of the view that people who are sucked into the orbit of the machine tend to be emotionally different from the rest of us. Turkle's argument in the early 1980s was essentially that engineers tended to think of themselves as slightly autistic because of the romantic reaction in our culture; the Asperger's data seems to suggest that engineers do in fact tend to fall onto the autism spectrum more often than the rest of us.

Furthermore, the overlap between Aspies and fans of science fiction, fantasy lit, role-playing games, and video games is huge, says Attwood, "both in appreciation and writing."

"Sci-fi is a mixture of science and imagination. For the little kids who are fascinated by *Star Wars* and those who join NASA, it very much suits their mind-set," he says. "The assumption is that people with Asperger's don't have imagination—oh, yes they do, but it tends to be a solitary pursuit and not a social pursuit."

Aspies will also fall far afield from engineering. "In Hollywood you get as many people with Asperger's as in Silicon Valley," Attwood tells me, and I respond with a kind of sputtering interrogative noise that means, "Who?" I've heard of one prominent comedy writer generally acknowledged to have it, but nothing like computer-industry levels. "Just my clinical experience," he says. "Not Tom Cruise types, but a very intelligent way of coping with social confusion is to find people who are successful with social interaction and imitate them and then use drama classes to learn how to act.

"I've known several politicians with Asperger's, including a very significant one in Australia," adds Attwood. "One of the things the person with Asperger's has is a strong sense of social justice. The tendency is to be on the right rather than the left; it's more dogmatic and rigid." Aspies, believes Attwood, "have often been used by their party because of their honesty and interest and integrity so they can be the logical front person." Thomas Jefferson is one of the historical figures Attwood considers a candidate for an Asperger's diagnosis.

Despite the efforts and goodwill of psychologists like Attwood, who want people on the autism spectrum to be diagnosed but not stigmatized, it seems nearly inevitable that some social damage will always accompany a diagnosis. There's a scene in Mark Haddon's novel *The Curious Incident of the Dog in Night-Time,* narrated by a teenager who could be described as having serious social issues, having Asperger's syndrome, or being autistic, depending on the diagnostician. He's on a school bus full of children on the way to the special school he attends, children who would have once been called "mentally handicapped," "retarded," or "mentally ill" but who are now more neutrally referred to as having "special needs." The kids from the normal school run alongside the bus and scream "Special needs! Special needs!" The point is that stigma doesn't accrue only to people who are given inherently stigmatic labels. Any label becomes stigmatic when it means that you go to a different school or turn from a central hallway into the room set aside for children who have needs beyond or different from what other children have.

Asperger's is a condition that usually includes a deficit of empathy, and, by implication, social skills. Having social skills means having the ability to make people like you. You can't erase stigma by saying, "Don't dislike me because I'm bad at making you like me." You can't achieve intimacy by saying, "You're going to have to work harder to achieve intimacy with me, because intimacy doesn't come easily to me." You'd have to be exceptionally rich and good-looking to pull it off. Asperger's syndrome is not like dyslexia, a disorder (or neurological makeup) that can be compensated for once it's diagnosed. A dyslexic gets extra time to complete tests, extra help with papers from the writing center. His teachers can be expected to understand if he has problems with arithmetic or sentence structure. But Asperger's syndrome describes a preference for the rational, a problem understanding what people are trying to tell you, and a tendency toward physical movements that don't correspond to any conventional notion of sexiness or grace. How do you compensate for that? Nobody's figured out a system. When Craig Nicholls of the Vines hits a photographer and gets a reduced sentence because he's been diagnosed with Asperger's, no one knows what kind of rules are in the offing. Isn't songwriter/rock star a fundamentally empathetic rather than rational profession? And isn't it a line of work in which Nicholls was for six months quite successful? Furthermore, nobody is really sure if Asperger's is something that should be compensated for at all; intense focus and a tendency toward systemic thinking are usually desirable qualities in an employee, and Aspies often speculate whether Bill Gates is one of their own.

All of which begs the question: if you've been informed you have Asperger's, what are you supposed to do? Of course there are Aspies who should be diagnosed and counseled. But an overly broad application of the Asperger's diagnosis is dangerous for nerds. If Thomas Jefferson, among other things an effective leader and tireless personal correspondent, Mozart, Glenn Gould, Ludwig Wittgenstein, and Alan Turing can be suspected of having had Asperger's (these names are all listed as possible "Asperger's Achievers" on Tony Attwood's Web site), why not just about anyone? Given that being diagnosed with Asperger's can worsen rather than ameliorate social isolation because of the self-consciousness it creates, does the potential good that comes from a diagnosis of mild Asperger's outweigh the potential harm?

Attwood's hope is that we're entering an age in which having Asperger's syndrome isn't a major obstacle to social acceptance because being a nerd isn't a major obstacle to social acceptance. "It's a relatively modern prejudice," he says, of the hostility toward nerds. "Because [video] games are so popular in the general population, *nerd* may not be such a derogatory term anymore."

To play devil's advocate with Attwood: even as magazine writers and T-shirts cheer for nerds and their economic ascendancy, have we begun to diagnose as a disorder the behavior that made people nerds when we were in elementary school? At the very least, we're recasting behavior once considered merely eccentric and sometimes unattractive as evidence of hard-wired neurological difference. There are nerdy kids being told their behavior isn't a choice or a set of temporary compulsions but something essential, a permanent condition, one that precludes social life as the rest of us experience it, but that this condition isn't a bad thing—Thomas Jefferson might have had it.


Is there an ideological component to the autism spectrum? More specifically, what is the ideology behind calling a lack of empathy a disorder (or a difference that requires special attention)? Normal, honorable masculinity in agrarian nineteenth-century America and Europe was not tied to empathy—being a good man meant you could support your family by farming or plying a trade, and that you could fight in a war. The health manuals for young men emphasized abstinence from sex because sex could sap energy and focus. Even the Theodore Roosevelt–era emphasis on displaying leadership qualities and manly vigor didn't hold proper masculinity to include empathy. The traits that the *DSM-IV* and the other diagnostic systems attribute to Asperger's—friendships oriented around activities, a preoccupation with the "creative" over the "cooperative" (Attwood's terms), an inability to "express love to the degree loved ones expect" (Attwood again)—might have been considered unusual in women back then but not in men.

The idea that having a capacity for empathy, for expressing and understanding emotion, is part of being a normal male is fundamentally contemporary and a way of asking that men learn a traditionally feminine virtue. When men were in an unquestioned position of control in the economy—when the bedrock of the nuclear family was a single male wage, a flow of income largely unavailable to women—there was less force compelling men to make themselves attractive mates through understanding the feelings of others and expressing affection. The Asperger's population is 90 percent male; it's likely that one reason Asperger's got "discovered" and then "boomed" is that the rest of us have been slowly revising our expectations of men.

Because people with Asperger's can only be considered unusual within the context of social norms, and because Asperger's has its advantages, there is an increasingly strident and organized Aspie Pride movement. Based in England, a group called Aspies for Freedom opposes the "pitying charity" of those organizations, such as Cure Autism Now, who would eradicate disorders on the autism spectrum. For now, there's a middle way between that of the pride advocates and the "curebies"—why not try to treat social problems while exploiting gifts? The problem is that, for years now, the pride movement has with dread anticipated a prenatal test for autism, a development that could conceivably take place soon, according to experts like Baron-Cohen. Since 80 percent of Down's syndrome fetuses are aborted, this would be a watershed moment for both the people who want autism-spectrum conditions cured and those who want them to stay around. As one of Aspies for Freedom's founders, Gareth Nelson, told the *Guardian* newspaper, "I don't want to get to be an old man and know that there will be no more people like me being born."

It must be bittersweet when your state of being goes from having a somewhat insulting informal name, like *nerd,* to having an honest-to-God diagnosis that attracts the attention of well-meaning psychologists and neurologists. In another era, Nelson might have gotten through life being thought of as a boffin, like Turing and the other English nerds who broke German codes at Bletchley Park during World War II (Churchill is said to have called Bletchley "the goose that laid the golden eggs and never cackled"). Because he lives in this era, Nelson has self-knowledge and fellowship on one hand, and the prospect of having his fellows eliminated on the other; if not filtered out in prenatal phase, then normalized, to some extent, by treatment.

Since nerdiness and Asperger's have so much in common, the specter that looms before Nelson confronts all nerds, in a milder form. Will nerdiness—not just the compulsion toward systemic thinking, but the eccentricities that have made the nerd character a staple of pop culture—become even less "normal" if they resemble an increasingly well-known and rigorously treated disorder? For all that Aspie camaraderie, I'd bet there are Aspies out there who'd rather be thought of as nerds.

# pure pwnage

"RAPE!"

"Raaaaaaaape!"

"R A P E."

These are three of the posts on Major League Gaming's message board that use *rape* as a synonym for *sweet* or *awesome*. If the function of teenage slang is to alienate adults, *rape* gets the job done efficiently. Plus it's a rank paste that holds the video-game dork family together; a young man who says "rape" when something awesome occurs is going to face challenges getting laid, and, assuming a dearth of sexual activity leaves you with more time to play Halo, *rape* keeps gamers in the fold.

But I'm being cruel to children on a message board now, even if they are misogynist children. *Rape* makes a certain sense, given that the satisfactions of video gaming tend to derive from repetitive acts of violence. You see the most acute euphoria descend on a player when he's got his opponent(s) directly in his sights and he opens fire by mashing the "shoot" button on the controller as rapidly as possible, watching the enemy writhe in the stream of ammo. *Rape* is an analogy.

The meanings of *rape* extend beyond *good*—it's also a flexible verb. ("Apparently Robot Chicken raped this clip from samster"—Counter-Strike Forum, June, 2006.) More important, *rape* is one term in an assault-oriented lexicon. Video-game-related Web sites are full of entries like this one, from purepwnage.com:

> i pwn noobs like hard rite n my roomate has dis camera rite so hes all like "we can make a show lol" n im like dats the pwnage n stuff n hes like I no lol so im like ok film me noob n hes like ok so we did lololol
>
> then we lukd at it rite n were liek "ofmg stfu dats pure pwnage lol" so we made dis site n stuff rite n now were gonna b famose!!!!

This is a form of 1337, or leetspeak, which means "elite speak." It's a computer culture invention. Some versions of 1337, or 31337, the full numeric keypad spelling of "eleet," use more numerals, but 1337 is the contemporary manifestation of leetspeak built around video-game culture. The term *pwn,* for example, means "own," in the sense of "I own you," i.e., I killed you, beat you, dominated you. (It comes from a WarCraft game message that misspelled *own*—"this player is now pwned.") *Noob* is a variant of *newbie,* which originally meant somebody new to a game or online community and has evolved into an insult, or even a generic term for *guy,* like *dude, motherfucker,* or *nigga.* "I pwn noobs like hard rite" is the leet version of Eazy-E's "I just smoke motherfuckers like it ain't no thang." In both lines, the real meaning is probably more a general assertion of superiority than a specific claim—both the author of purepwnage and Eazy-E mean "I am a bad-ass" more than they mean "I beat novices by a wide margin," or "I shoot people with indifference."

Leetspeak dates back to the early bulletin board systems of the 1980s, when even short messages were so arduous to send that users truncated "you are" to "u r" and so on. Then the administrators of those boards started to clamp down on black-market traffic of pornography and software, so BBS users started to modify words so as to elude searches. *Porn* became "pr0n," and *hacker* became "hack0r" or "h4cker," which in turn had to be modified to "h4x0r." Even after messages became easy and fast to send, those terms started to evolve into nonutilitarian trash talk, popular in Multi-User Dungeons of the 1980s and '90s. (MUDs were early online role-playing games in which the players interacted purely through text.)

This new slang was developed largely by young men, and it has come to resemble, more than anything else, the language spoken by the delinquents in Anthony Burgess's *Clockwork Orange*. In that novel, a gang of sadistic teenage boys roams the streets of a ruined city, using what Burgess called a "Russified English." (In the movie those streets look a lot like the backgrounds in Halo: postindustrial noir monumentalism, cracked cement courtyards.) The words in that language are chiefly ones of violence: "I gave him a tolchok"; "a little of the old ultra-violent." Even the phrase for "I'm tired" suggests domination and beating—"I was fagged and fashed"—and the Russian word for "good," *khorosho,* becomes "horrorshow." Leetspeak shares with that fictional slang system a tendency to align good with violence and sex. In addition to *rape,* there's *slut* as a word for being skilled. "I slut at SSBM," for example, means "I'm good at Super

Smash Bros. Melee." One of the reasons to create your own elite slang system is to give yourself the feeling of belonging to a special, empowered group. The vocabulary of that language, in this case, reflects that will to power, the need for one-upmanship, the fantasy of violence and violent sex.

Today the high-ceilinged windowless maw that is the Meadowlands Expo Center in Secaucus, New Jersey, in the Harmon Meadow Center mall, is given over to the opening tournament of the 2006 season of Major League Gaming. The room is the kind of industrial cave that could work as a gay club or a warehouse for hot Alpine stereos. Since the main event is Halo 2, the meat of the sport is that you operate a futuristic soldier with a gun from a first-person perspective. You see the muzzle protruding upward from the bottom of the screen, firing out into the elegantly muted scenery. Since you can point this gun in any direction but you can't just put it down, the sensation that you are walking around with a huge black strap-on is difficult to transcend.

You usually play Halo at home, with an Xbox game console plugged into the Internet. The Web lets you play against anybody in the world also playing online, and you give yourself a tag—these are usually serious in a sci-fi way, like Flamesword65, or comic, like Poonanny. Without even going to a tournament, a player can garner some renown online; there are message boards full of gossip about the new top guns and the slipping former champions.

"From all walks of life" is how people here like to describe Halo players. This is hard to verify visually, because the hall is about 90 percent males between the ages of seven and twenty in baggy jeans and jerseys, but there are at least two four-woman Halo 2 teams here, such as PMS (Pandora's Mighty Soldiers, formerly Psychotic Men Slayerz), who wear baseball caps, shirts, and buttons with a logo that merges a rifle sight with the sign for female. There are also boys here who would not look out of place as extras on *The O.C.* or as bass players in Taking Back Sunday, with long hair swept forward across their faces, from the rear right quadrant of their heads, who have figured out the Eminem look is not ideal for making it with girls. They've found a way to lope through adolescence with a kind of fawn-legged grace.

But mostly these are not cool boys. Mostly these boys are nerds. This is not to say they have big glasses and high pants. There are some who would have been recognizable as nerds in my high school: XL heavy-metal T-shirt, slump, short, shapeless hair, unconvincing leer. But the outfit of the contemporary video-game nerd is a stab at a hip-hop ensemble. At some point in the legendary gangsta past, the baggy look alluded to the concealment of contraband, but now it's an attempt to hide the body. It's the adolescent equivalent of a comb-over, a look that's designed to cover a structural problem but worsens the whole package because it's clearly obfuscatory.

The clothes are not the only thing that makes the hall's appearance initially dispiriting. Whatever legitimate virtues might contribute to Halo 2's[1] greatness, however valid Halo 2's claim to being a sport, it's a challenge to look sporty, in any conventional sense of the word, while playing Halo 2. What with the lip curled in concentration, the hands in the lap working at maximum speed in repetitive motion, the fierce, dazed eyes staring straight ahead, dignity is elusive.

1. This event predates the Halo 3 release by over a year.

When you first enter the Major League Gaming tournament here at the Expo Center, you see long rows of boys poised in Halo 2 rapture. At the back of the hall there are three adjacent Jumbotron screens, each showing a different scene of combat in progress. There are bleachers set up before the Jumbotrons, where spectators can watch the championship matches unfold, and there are two rows of four monitors beneath the giant screens, swathed in red and blue lights.

But in a back corner of the room, a heady new movement is in bloom. Super Smash Bros. Melee may never be the main event at an MLG tournament. Super Smash Bros. Melee is, by design, kind of a children's game, or, as one of its top players, Wife, puts it, "a party game." It certainly doesn't project the stony serious- ness of Halo's scarred environments, where barely a single weed struggles through the cracks in the pavement. The backgrounds upon which the action unfolds in SSBM are Fisher-Price–like. There are oak trees whose mouths are prone to open in awe when somebody executes a difficult move, jungles where the palm leaves are as thick and soft as tongues. SSBM games don't go up on the Jumbotrons here, and nobody watches them from bleach- ers. Only one quarter of one of the rows of monitors in the hall belongs to SSBM. SSBM is a speck of volcanic activity in the gray wash of Halo 2.

In SSBM, you are an Italian guy (Mario or Luigi), a turtle mon- ster, a princess, Donkey Kong, or a Pokémon lump creature. You and your partner must bounce into the other team, knocking them offscreen. It's generally acknowledged that there is a West Coast style and an East Coast style, the former defensive, the latter offen- sive. This is plausible because SSBM is not an online game, like Halo 2, so there are regional networks of players who meet in physical locations. Beyond the difference in styles, there is an East Coast vs. West Coast rivalry.

There have been no shootings perpetrated in the Super Smash Bros. Melee East Coast vs. West Coast feud, but "somebody got hit once," at a tournament, SSBM players tell me. The New York SSBM tournament is an unusually loud event; the East Coast players are the more aggressive of the two regions, and the New York players are reputedly the most volatile in the country.

PC Chris is the only white kid in the Deadly Alliance, a group of New York City–area SSBMers who travel together and coach each other. He also happens to be one of the best-looking kids in the room, with thick dark hair in his eyes and porcelain skin, and there's a cult following around him, even if it exists mostly in the way people talk about him online. One player, Bach, has made an "I <3 PC Chris" T-shirt, and another kid here is actually wearing it.

One of the most stoical looking of the East Coasters is Wes, who wears a leather jacket and keeps a thick ponytail under a newsboy cap. He seems ambivalent about the fashion statement sported by the other black kid who's an East Coast player: the letters *QT* penned under his right eye.

Wes taps him on the shoulder. "Did you kill somebody?"[2]

"It's a name a girl gave me." The other kid shrugs, inching away.

Wes dismisses him with a wave. "Get out of here."

*QT* is an IM designation, Wes's target explains to me, meaning "cutie."

Soon after, I meet the Team Ben partnership who go by the

---

2. A street gang will tattoo a tear under an eye of one of its members to signify that he has committed murder.

names Husband and Wife. "They aren't gay," Bach explains to me. Wife's character is Princess Peach and Husband's character is Prince, who is Peach's husband in the game.

When we arrive at the final brackets, Ken and Isai face PC Chris and his partner, a kid who goes by the undiplomatic name of I-Dick-A. This is it: the New Yorkers of the Deadly Alliance are ready to represent for their side, hoping for an upset. Every jump-and-bump combo that New York executes is a coup, met with wide-eyed excitement ("HOOOOH!").

"Yee-ah!" says one of the white onlookers, when New York carries off a joint attack.

"YEE-ah!" says one of the Deadly Alliance guys. "Whatever that shit means."

Then the mood starts to change. Ken and Isai actually appear to be falling to Chris and I-Dick-A. The Deadly Alliance guy's satirical YEE-ahs give way, and he lets out an "Oh, *shit*."

"Ha! Hoh! HOH!"

Finally, jaws drop and baseball caps come off. Chris and I-Dick-A have won. PC Chris and I-Dick-A stand and embrace, and a New York kid yells and waves his NYC cap in the air. In response the Deadly Alliance's manager waves his signature old-school Nintendo power glove, and his players thud into him to hug and rejoice.

In the course of the weekend, Halo 2 events will fill the bleachers at the back of the hall. The MLG is determined to make this a visually compelling sport, and so Sundance DiGiovanni, MLG's founder, takes up a mic before the big matches and leads a warm-up in which the audience practices compelling reactions before the USA

Network rolls its cameras. It becomes clear, watching New York take on LA in SSBM, that the "Smash" crowd needs no such encouragement. But the cameras remain on the special lighting, the Halo 2, Red Bull's cross-promo banners. Smash seems to be a real sporting community here, behind all the rape talk and the press-release language, still largely undetected, marginalized at MLG Pro events and uncorrupted by professionalism.

This is because Smash is a culture of people who have to get together in the same place (generally a basement in the suburbs, as it happens) to play their game. Halo 2, by contrast, is just as easily played online as in a live tournament hall like this one, and that accounts for vast differences. Sundance DiGiovanni has to goad Halo 2 audiences into becoming good live crowds, cheering at the right moment; with Smash, this is not necessary. Smash needs in-the-flesh gatherings to have tournaments, so it has regional identities, like hip-hop, and regional feuds, like hip-hop. Halo 2 doesn't, which drains the blood out of its live events, no matter how juicy the vivisections onscreen.

# the graying of
# the old-school nerd

### meeting #3518

When you enter the Los Angeles Science Fantasy Society compound, the first noises you hear are those of middle-aged men playing video games. It's an unfamiliar sound—deep, wizened voices saying the words they are saying. The closest thing is a Clint Eastwood movie.

Whiskey voice: "We've got to get out of here."

Nasal: "Go south, go—"

Sonorous: "You think you can get around me, do you? Well, how about some of this?"

The jungly wires of the computer game room come into view after you've edged past the bookcase full of paperbacks on your right, and the scene fully reveals itself a step later. If you've lived with drug addicts, there's something familiar in the way all evidence of human effort is concentrated in one area while the rest of the space shows neglect; the five screens dance with activity, blue-white, and the men hunch before the screens, while machinery threatens to fall on their heads from overcrowded shelves. Also familiar: the enviable degree of focus. The men have gray hair and wrinkled foreheads, but their voices carry a hint of dreamy contentment. Magazines, books, and meals cover most surfaces.

The first person I meet is Scratch, who looks exactly like Santa Claus except for what appear to be two small knives holstered to his belt.

"This is a social club for people who for the most part have no social skills," Scratch explains. The Los Angeles Science Fantasy Society was founded in 1934, and since the 1970s it has owned its own pair of one-story rectangular buildings, joined by a cement courtyard and marked by an illuminated white sign containing its shield logo, which in turn contains a comet and a rocket ship and suggests the insignia of a military spacecraft.

"My interests include science, books, anime, and films," says Scratch. "Have you heard of stop-motion animation?" he asks, suddenly changing course. He points to a poster for the stop-motion feature *The Wizard of Speed and Time* autographed by the filmmaker in gold ink for the club.

Before I finish saying "*Clash of the Titans,*" he begins to tell me about the frames per second of *The Wizard of Speed and Time,* so I'm not forced to feign expertise. There are also posters for *Sky Captain and the World of Tomorrow* and *Chicken Little.*

At the regular Thursday night meetings, we all sit facing two elected officials at a desk. Behind them is a dry-erase board, which says "Meeting #3518." It's a full house. Most people have the bemused expressions you have around your family. It's largely male, but not manly or even latently gay, except for Scratch giving the man with large glasses and Velcro sneakers in front of him an un-inhibited neck and shoulder massage (the origin of his name?), cradling the dome of the man's head like a grapefruit in one large hand and working his fingers into the ripe pink flesh of his neck.

The recipient of the massage, which lasts through the entirety of the first two-hour-long meeting I attend, is Jerry Pournelle, a libertarian political writer and the coauthor, with Larry Niven, of *Lucifer's Hammer*, a sci-fi bestseller in which a comet strikes earth and survivalists are forced to fend off cannibal African Americans. He believes mean intellectual ability among races is "spectacularly unequal" and advocates allowing "eggheads" to sequester themselves from "skill-set" types.[1] The prevailing philosophy about beliefs like this at LASFS is, as Scratch puts it, "I don't believe in little green men. There's a lady here who really does believe in little green men. And that's fine."

LASFS, pronounced "Lasfus," is in North Hollywood, in the Valley. It sits across Burbank Boulevard from an Affiliated Property Craftspersons Local 44 and a business called Fangs that specializes in custom dental-acrylic pointy tooth-caps for vampire lovers. The meeting room has brown carpeting and fake wood walls, and on Sundays there are five folding tables spread throughout on which members play strategy and role-playing games.

The minutes at the Thursday meetings are read by a man with curly black hair and moons under his eyes and a Dark Realms T-shirt, and they are read in an English accent. At first I wonder if it's a real English accent.

---

1. From Pournelle's blog, The View from Chaos Manor: "The mean IQs of different races are not only unequal but in some cases spectacularly unequal . . . The ability to manipulate symbols is unequally distributed across the races."

One of the older members in the wings turns to another and asks a whispered question. The other, who has a beautiful bottle-green tattoo of a compasslike symbol on his wrist, replies, loud enough to be heard halfway across the room, "No, it's his British acting."

The minutes read, the man in the Dark Realms shirt goes back to being an American nerd.

## journey into space

After a reading of the minutes of the previous meeting of the Los Angeles Science Fantasy Society, there is an accounting of the dead. A gray-haired man in a white lab coat, the kind a mad scientist would wear, sixty-something, stands.

"We have lost Syd Raymond," he says. Raymond was the voice of Heckle and Jeckle, the cartoon crows; his credits are listed. "We have lost Marty Nodell, who cocreated the Green Lantern," he continues. Jerry Pournelle offers a short tribute to Jeane Kirkpatrick, who also died this week. "Mr. Heinlein," he explains, (there is no need to say "Robert" to establish he is talking about the sci-fi colossus), unsuccessfully urged her to run for president.

"First a moment of silence," says the man in the white lab coat. Silence. "And a laugh"—everybody sings out a "ha ha ha." "And a 'wowww.'" He points to the sky, suggesting wonderment at a flying object. The congregation responds in kind. For each name called out the ritual is repeated: silence, then "ha ha ha," then "wowww."

This ritual, which takes place at the beginning of each LASFS meeting, is basically, but not exactly, a death roll. The word written on the dry-erase board at the back is *Saints,* with the names of the subjects beneath it, some of whom are living. At one meeting, the first saint is a deceased NASA scientist, Dan Alderson. Like Quakers in a meetinghouse, the LASFS members stand up to express the thoughts that descend upon them, as they consider their brothers— "He was the sanest mad scientist I know," someone says. Jerry Pournelle brings up the fact that he called a device the Alderson Drive in his own *Lucifer's Hammer* ("a book which has sold 45 million copies worldwide"). The man in the white coat reminds us Alderson could have made three times his salary elsewhere if he'd left NASA, but he was dedicated to the space program. The feel of the meeting is not so much clubby as congregational; in some sense, even if nobody says so, it's a spiritual group.

There are a few teenagers at LASFS meetings. They stick to themselves, pairing off to play video games or smoke in the courtyard of the compound. A new girl, a teenager in a black hoodie and wire-rimmed glasses, stands up to be formally introduced, but most of them stick to the front room, talking about the best and worst scenes in *Superman,* playing computer games.

One of the subjects that usually come up when you talk to long-standing members here is "the graying of fandom." (Scratch brought this up maybe ten minutes after I first walked in the door of LASFS.) I find in the archives of the recently eulogized Fred Patten an account of a LASFS meeting in the 1980s. "Average attendance today is about one hundred twenty-five per week. There's high turnover; most attendees range from high-school age to their late twenties. I joined when I was in college in 1960 and I'm now one of the LASFS old-timers . . ." Now, of course, the middle-aged and the elderly are the rank and file, and the high-school-to-college demographic is a fringe. The people who would have been voracious readers of sci-fi and fantasy in previous generations are spending their time other ways. Computer and console games offer the same themes (adventure, battle, groups of heroic characters with diverse abilities on a quest to thwart a force of evil). They demand less time than books, they link hundreds of thousands of players through the Internet, and they are increasingly portable. The clubhouse becomes endangered.

The LASFS clubhouse is in an ugly building, from the inside especially. But it's also a warm and serious place. It's hard to think of another location in Los Angeles so welcoming to outsiders that's not a temple on Sunset Boulevard with uniformed novices handing out brochures on the sidewalk. More important, LASFS is about people in a room talking, largely about books. It has a real lending library with a helpful librarian, and a devoted assortment of readers who read its books. Like so many things that are decrepit to the point where they might in theory be eulogized, LASFS makes a eulogy rise in my throat. I want it to hang on.

More precisely, I want the meeting room to hang on. The space between the meeting room in back and the video-game room in the front is huge. It's the difference between a room built around conversation and a room built around a chain of screens.

In Grand Theft Auto and other simulations of real life, there's no difference in importance between blowing things up and getting haircuts.[2] The effect of the game is to put trivialities (decisions regarding the line of your fade, whether you have a necklace) on the same scale as massive explosions that kill the meddlesome passersby. It's not the violence of the game that's distinctive so much as the way it eliminates proportion—everything becomes a series of choices calculated to generate fun.

2. See George Trow's remarks on television and the erosion of the distinction between trivial and monumental events in *Within the Context of No Context*.

Trying very hard to have fun: this is the cloud that hovers over both the video-game room at LASFS and the Major League Gaming events. There's no real need for the participants or spectators to sit in the same room at MLG events, and you feel that lack of need. The knowledge that there is absolutely zero difference between sitting three feet away from somebody playing Halo and playing Halo with headsets in different states—this is what makes MLG so sad. You can watch a mediocre snowboarder get air in person and feel you've had a rich spectator experience. With Halo the visual spectacle isn't the thumbs; it's the imaginary men with guns in the ruined battlefield. You can watch it just as well over the Internet. The reasons to be in the MLG hall are not real.

The reasons to be in the LASFS meeting room are real. Sainting isn't a rational activity; it's just the necessary ritual of a put-upon tribe. The focus is the suffering, the mortality, the choice of how to spend a life. Whatever you say about sci-fi fans, they have an acute sense of the monumental. A pretty good definition of sci-fi, in fact, is fiction that focuses exclusively on monumental events: plagues, comets, interspecies wars, the return of the dinosaurs. In its absolute disregard for anything like clear surfaces or remodeling or lighting or nice smells, the clubhouse devotes itself exclusively to big deals—the first contact with alien races is depicted over and over again, like the crucifixion. The heroes fight whole ill-intentioned planets with laser guns and swords.

LASFS members have a sense of the difference between trivial and huge. Enormity is sacred. That's why they make the "wowww" sound when they come together to mourn their dead.

# coronation,
# or why group nerd events
# are necessary

During the five years of my life when I played Dungeons & Dragons on and off—age eight to age thirteen—there was drama. Somebody's single mother would take a new boyfriend into her condo on the edge of town, and that kid would have to go stay at another kid's house; somebody else's mother would be in the process of leaving his father, who had done something unspecified and evil, and so on. But our sessions began like this:

> FRIEND: *Long time no see, Benmeister.*
> ME: *Hey, how are you?*
> FRIEND: *All right. I'm really tired these days. I'm living with my*
> *mom again instead of at Marty's house.*
> ME: *Yeah, moms are tiring.*
> FRIEND: *Nice—you've got a green twelve-sided now.*

ME: *Yeah, green like the lizard that's going to gnaw your bones this*
   *adventure.*
FRIEND: *Hoh.*
ME: *Ah, you laugh now.*

What brought us together was a game, not a promise of mutual understanding. So far as we were aware.

What was it about assuming the role of pretend characters that
was so attractive? Was it an escape hatch from our deficient real
lives? Was the monstrous reality of D&D (and Middle Earth Role
Playing, and the Teenage Mutant Ninja Turtles & Other Strangeness role-playing game) a metaphor for the unarticulated terror we
felt when we considered the conflicts among adults that shaped our
lives?

Thinking about the nature of the role-playing-game impulse, I
drive to the official coronation of a monarch of the southern California chapter of the Society for Creative Anachronism (SCA), oth-
erwise known as the Kingdom of Caid. This is the e-mail I have
received from Karin Burgess, a Realtor helping to plan the ceremony:

Greetings Benjamin,

My name is Lady Muiriath mac Labhruinn, Reevess of Dun Or and
the Feast Stewart. We would be delighted to have you attend our
event. It would be greatly appreciated that you do dress within the
perimeters of our Society. This is a Kingdom level event, and as
such, there will be many high ranking members in attendance . . .

Yours in Service,
Lady Muiriath mac Labhruinn

Reevess, Barony of Dun Or

Order of the Harp Agent

Order of the Dolphin

Order of the Duelist

Recipient of the Crossed Swords

KKA: Karin Burgess

The twin towns of the Antelope Valley, Lancaster and Palmdale, offer vast, flat desert views dominated by a Lowe's and a Costco, which each cover football fields upon football fields of square footage, their parking lots approaching the size of Times Square. It looks like a parody of Midwestern spaciousness. When we reach Lancaster, we stop at a gas station for water and in the gas station mini-mart two women in Renaissance gowns are buying snacks. A guy in robes knocks over a Slippery When Wet sign with his cloak on the way out, and I pick it up for him, so he bows in gratitude.

Today, the SCA claims thirty thousand members across the globe, assigning every corner of the earth an identity as a kingdom or principality (Australia and New Zealand, for example, comprise the Kingdom of Lochac). While the SCA does have a fighting component, it's dedicated to replicating any aspect of life from AD 600–1600 that interests its members. SCA members don't, generally speaking, play illiterate peasants who die of infection at age five. But they do sew clothing, forge armor, practice medicine, and establish elaborate hierarchies of nobles, barons, and kings. The Massachusetts-based queen of one SCA kingdom explained to the *Christian Science Monitor* that she spent about twelve hours a week on the phone resolving problems among her subjects.

The SCA spread gradually outward from northern California,

today part of the West Kingdom, which also includes Nevada, Alaska, Japan, Korea, and the Pacific Rim. The Kingdom of the East, which includes eastern Pennsylvania, eastern New York, Delaware, New Jersey, and New England, was created in 1968. (A kingdom is officially established when somebody is crowned its king or queen.) The Middle Kingdom, which contains most of the Midwest, was born a year later. Atenveldt, or Arizona, came around in 1971. Southern California and the Southeast followed in 1978, and the rest of the world capitulated over the following two decades.

The coronation takes place two minutes away, in a Knights of Columbus Hall. Across Avenue M from the hall is a patch of flat desert dotted with brush and Joshua trees. It runs uninterrupted to a spine of blue mountains.

Outside the hall, eight merchants have erected tents of purple and white cloth. Everybody is "in garb," in the parlance of the SCA, except for two young men, one of whom wears a backward fitted baseball cap, who browse through the swords. The swords sit on wooden racks outside one of the tents, and look real. They have metal blades two inches wide and two to three feet long, with hilts and pommels emblazoned with runes and dragon heads. The desert sun is blinding when it hits a blade flashing in the air.

Standing by one of the merchandise stands, three of the men start to sing part of "If I Were a Rich Man" in unison. Digital photographs are taken. A woman by the sword-stands digs in a purple Snoopy bag for something to mollify her peasant child, who is crying. Three women talk about fabrics while three men chuckle among themselves with steins of grog at the opposite end of the parking lot.

Now the future king and queen of Caid take the stage. The king is large and lithe and red-maned and heavily muscled. "He is built for fighting with sticks," a fighter will tell me later, in slightly awed tones. There are freckles on his bare shoulders.

The queen is slim, with long black hair and kind dark eyes. Her tiara looks natural on her head. She's a belly-dancing teacher in the area who often works in a shop owned by other SCA members.

"You know I'm a cheerleader," she says, "so let's hear it for the Kingdom of Caid!"

"Huzzah!" cry the assembled.

"Hip hip," she says.

"Huzzah!"

They do this a few more times.

"As you know," says the queen, "here in Dun Or [the Antelope Valley] we have a lot of active members of the military. I personally have friends in both Iraq and Afghanistan . . . So may our military members spread word of our kingdom in foreign lands." The queen gives the military subjects American flag ribbons to wear on their doublets.

That night I go to a party at a house in Beachwood Canyon in Los Angeles inhabited by several TV writers who are about to get kicked out by the landlord. A single rocket-powered grenade directed at this structure would have an appreciable effect on the funniness of next year's prime-time lineup, and this knowledge endows the party with a feeling of national importance. You can go a good ten minutes here without hearing a sentence that does not employ irony in a way that would confuse my grandparents.

"Fun? No, this is all boring Harvard people."

"The next people who get this house are going to get haunted, like in *The Shining*. They'll open a door and see two comedy writers butt-fucking."

"Hey, guys: let's go to the bathroom and snort coke like those whores over there."

At this party, any duel or a coronation takes place in a mist, hard to detect and impossible to be sure of. Officially, nobody is in charge. Nobody reports to anybody. There's room for anxiety about status because nobody's status is settled. The questions that arise, never voiced, are unanswerable. Who is most successful and most esteemed? Nobody can visibly best somebody else and shake their hand and be done with it. Favorable opinion sidles up against one person, then falls away to sidle up against another, and these defeats and victories are invisible. Some part of you longs to see them, to be able to point at somebody and say, there is the king.

This feeling isn't distinct to gatherings of writers or to Los Angeles; a coronation is a temporary relief from the paranoia of a deceptive everyday life.

Which brings me back to me and the other boys skipping over the major news items of our family lives to get straight to the new twelve-sided die. What we needed was a flight into order and transparency, and in Dungeons & Dragons, boffing and computers, we found it. It was no coincidence, I think, that we generally came to D&D from home lives that tended toward the unpredictable and confounding. We wanted a place where you knew where you stood, where everything was laid out so you could see it. In the fantasies we made together, you weren't always king, but you could always point to him.

■

The February after my first SCA excursion, I drive to Estrella War, which takes place every year in a desert park outside of Phoenix. Two medieval women are assigned as tour guides to me and to my friend, who is holding a video camera. In a white golf cart, they chauffeur us through a thousand-bannered city sprung up in the yellow dust. First we see a neighborhood devoted to the arts and sciences of AD 600–1600. Three women bake bread in white clay ovens shaped like hedgehogs. One of them, Sharon, tells me about how her son called her from Afghanistan to tell her about the amazing bread Afghans bake in primitive earthen kitchens.

"I said, 'I think you've already had it before.'"

Nearby, Master Johann, a woodmaker, eats his lunch on a wooden plate, sipping from a goblet, surrounded by wares. There's a toolbox modeled on one from the eleventh century unearthed in Europe, a knife on his belt he made himself, a small arsenal of wooden tools scattered throughout the tent. His persona, he explains, stroking his beard, eyes partially obscured by a cloth hood, is a Germanic artisan of Celtic heritage.

These are the peaceful creatures of the SCA, nerds among nerds, delving into technical crafts when they could have chosen to live as knights or mercenaries. Whether or not Master Johann thinks of himself as one of the SCA's brainy members, the fighters of the SCA are alive to the fact that they are the frat brothers. They call themselves "stick jocks," a stick being an SCA weapon like a rattan sword or spear. Sure, stick jocks wear shields with meticulously painted heraldry, and train for knighthood, and respect the hierarchies within their kingdoms and baronies, but they also kick back in Johnny Cash T-shirts with Miller High Life and Marbs, telling what are known in the SCA as "No shit, I was there" stories—tales of battle.

This sounds delusional until you see the actual warfare at Estrella War. About a thousand men on each side march at one another with rattan spears and swords covered with tape, protected by helmets, shields, and chain mail that are essentially real, made of metal. Your eyes sting from the dust, and when you hear the sound of a roving army of "heavies," you understand why they are called heavies. It's the sound of a giant metal porcupine uncurling itself from a nap.

The pep talk:

"It's ankle-biting time, so don't fuck up!"

"There's a bounty placed on Cedric, okay? So watch out for him."

"Remember: intensity."

After the armies muster under the flags of their respective kingdoms they start to pound rhythmically on the desert floor with their weapons, like the orcs at the beginning of the Battle for Helm's Deep in Peter Jackson's adaptation of *The Two Towers*. They charge and roar. For ten seconds, you hear only the din of their concerted movements forward. Then, as the beasts collide in the midpoint, there's a new sound: rival cop armies in riot gear fracturing against each other. The cries are semiecstatic—the bloodlust collected over a million beatings in junior high corridors, I imagine, rushing into the desert daylight, screaming its head off.

There are men who run herd between the battle and reality, holding poles to keep the armed limbs inside a defined battlefield. They are the only ones who never seem in danger of falling—anyone else could go tumbling over his lance and shield, caught upside the helmet by a berserker, uprooted by a column charge. A column charge is what happens when a group of fighters packs together, puts its six-to-twenty shields forward and its six-to-twenty heads down, and runs, as a flying fist, into the ranks of the enemy, aiming to penetrate as deeply as possible. The effect of a column charge is confusion—it disorients the opponents' front ranks and forces them to turn backward to subdue the human projectiles in their midst. Then the rest of the chargers' own army exploits the distraction to go in for the kill.

"It's pretty much a suicide mission," a winded column charger from the Phoenix area tells me. "You have to totally commit to it. You have to push in as far as you can and kill as many people as you can so that the people behind you can do the same."

This stoic exemplifies everything that I admired in the stick jocks—the courage, the good-natured exhaustion that comes from a day of exercise, the loyalty to the group, the tolerance for real physical suffering.

Smoking and nursing beers and waters, three stick jocks talk to me about the battle that evening before everyone hits the showers. They give me a beer, a chair, and lunch. More precisely, they give me a beer and a chair, and one of their girlfriends, actually dressed like you'd think a medieval wench would dress, prepares and serves us each a sandwich on a stiff high-quality paper plate with another plate placed over it to keep the ants from the desert at bay.

One of them shows me a wound. It's a wide-ranging tumescence the color of apple-raspberry juice, raised half a centimeter above the healthy flesh. "Somebody hit me with something like a tree—pow!—and that felt all kinds of wonderful," he says. He describes what it takes to stop a column charge: "Plant your front foot down and keep your shield up and just say: 'Bam! I don't think so! Not coming through this way.'"

The types usually considered to embody the essence of America are cowboys, baseball players, and gangsters. What is distinctly

American about them is the way they create an alternate world where they can construct their own land with its own rules and its own status pyramid. The original American dream, for the pilgrims, for the immigrant hordes, was to construct a new country that gave them the respect and possibility the old one couldn't. Isn't that what the SCA is doing?

You can almost convince yourself that a patch of desert is its own green-breasted continent; it's easy to ignore the signs of the real world when you're nestled in an army of fellow believers. Thus ensconced, you can almost convince yourself that you are the man you've constructed in your imagination. The SCA spans the globe, and is said to have an enthusiastic Ukrainian chapter, but it started in America, after all.

I follow the column-charge guys to the mobile shower trailers, where the stick jocks drink Irish whiskey and sing a jig: "Behind the door / Her father keeps a cannon / He keeps it in the springtime / And in the month of May."

Then a call and response: "Far away! *Far away!* Far away! *Far away!*"

Are these really nerds? Yes, but they're nerds who have banded together and found a way to make themselves non-nerds within a separate universe. "We were dorks in high school," one of the stick jocks tells me. "But we're dorks who can kick your ass." They've put the game of pretend in a logical grid of titles, allegiances, and hierarchies, but they've also made it outdoorsy and valorous. Whether it's Master Johann plying his skills as an independent craftsman, or the defenders of the queen fallen on the field, they've found a way to solve the old problems that Muscular Christianity and the Victorian sports advocates with their physique buttons sought to address.

There's a shot in *Welcome to the Dollhouse* where Todd Solondz's camera pans from right to left across a suburban front yard. The object it follows is a little girl in a pink tutu, twirling over the grass in an attempt at ballet. She twirls nearer and nearer to the garage, where her teenage brother's band practices. The band is more an imitation of a rock band than a rock band, because her brother plays the clarinet, and there is no singer. The dancing, of course, is an imitation of ballet. Both the band and the dancer are lost in fantasies of being engaged in glamorous creative endeavor, and the landscape in which they are situated is the opposite of a glamorous setting: a street full of ranch houses in New Jersey. The band wants to be the Rolling Stones—they're trying to play "(I Can't Get No) Satisfaction"—and the little girl wants to be a ballerina. They would never see themselves as having anything in common with each other. But they are both willfully submerged in a fantasy that provides an escape from their actual conditions and prospects.

The state this scene depicts is one that can't last—it's pulsing with the likelihood of its own demise. For now, the boys in the band can cling, rightfully, to a limited optimism; as one band member puts it to the others, "Come on, guys. This is our first practice. Think how the Rolling Stones must have sounded on their first practice." And he's right. They're fifteen; if they actually stay together and continue to practice, and keep up with what's happening in New York, and learn how to dress just a little bit better, they may well be a formidable rock band when they're all twenty, or at least when they're twenty-three. If the little girl starts taking ballet lessons and finds the wherewithal to practice as spiritedly as she messes around, there's no reason why she shouldn't become a dancer. But, as we can assume from looking at the adults in *Welcome to the Dollhouse,* this probably won't happen. Sloth and fear of failure will assert themselves, and they'll become salesmen, computer technicians, and home-makers. The fantasy remains an escape because it's also a viable aspiration—in twirling or in playing "Satisfaction," the children can imagine they're preparing to become their future selves. Eventually, the imagined futures will become implausible, and the fantasy will have to die.

The distinctive thing about so many nerds I've met is their willingness to pursue a dream version of their lives even when that dream isn't a plausible aspiration. Playing Sir Guillaume doesn't have anything to do with reinventing yourself through ambition. It has no careerist or pragmatic component. It's imitating the thing you most want to be, and that only, with no hope of the world outside your own head and your own group of friends coming round to accept it as the truest version of who you are. It sustains the band scene from *Welcome to the Dollhouse* into a phase of life that for others must bring with it the band scene's end.

# why do people like
# dungeons & dragons and fake swords?

## rules

In the Middle Ages, people said what was on their minds and took orders, right? In a primitive sketch of a hierarchical feudal society, status would be doled out at birth. Thanes would be absolutely loyal to kings in exchange for food and shelter. Upward economic mobility would not be accessible to serfs, and a commoner wouldn't have a shot at becoming more popular than a lord, so there wouldn't be much social conniving. People would know their places and say what needed to be said. Everyday interactions would involve phrases like, "Ho, traveler—state your purpose here. We will harm no man who comes in peace."

Of course the Middle Ages were not like this. But the medieval times that children of the late twentieth century encountered in movies from *Robin Hood* to *The Sword in the Stone* were jolly, formal, and stilted. They were the opposite of a contemporary American high school, where being accepted demanded a sensitivity to social cues, and you had to be able to discern how people wanted you to dress, what jokes you could crack, whom you were supposed to befriend, and whom you were supposed to avoid. The chivalrous culture surrounding swordplay and duels—as portrayed in movies and TV—appealed to kids who found the intricacies of contemporary high-school conversation challenging. It was an easy leap for them to embrace all things feudal.

A single thread runs through boffing, role-playing games like Dungeons & Dragons, ham-radio culture, the pop-culture version of the medieval world, and what J. R. R. Tolkien referred to as the American "cultus" surrounding *The Lord of the Rings:* the appeal of a heavily rule-bound universe. In the *Rings* trilogy, the tone of a character's speech and the content of that character's brain are determined mostly by a set of known quantities. If he's an elf, he's likely to speak and act with Beowulfian self-determination and noblesse oblige. If he's a hobbit he's likely to prioritize teacakes over wars against evil unless the prospect for domestic tranquility is on the line. If he's a dwarf he'll be truculent but stalwart and fundamentally well-intentioned. And if he's an orc he'll be implacably bad and prone to speak like a cockney thug. To be fair to Tolkien, there are creatures in his books far more subtly shaded than the ones outlined here, but with the publication of the *Rings* series during and after World War II and the increased interest in the *Rings* in the late 1960s and the '70s, nerd-dom developed a set of characters whose motives and moral compasses were easily understood and whose language was clear and non-allusive. These characters were easy for role-players to plug into different circumstances with an understanding of how they would behave. If role-players wanted to be people other than themselves, Tolkien and the fantasy writers who followed his lead were ready with templates that were universally understood in the nerd world.

There are other explanations, of course. "It's the romance," one longtime SCAer, Lyn Whitewolf, explained to me. "We had long-haired hippies, we had computer nerds. The FBI, J. Edgar Hoover's boys, they were checking us out. Soon they figured out what we were up to and we became a joke they'd give you as your first assignment. But I have a friend in the FBI, and when I asked him about whether they actually spied on us, he said, 'Sure—we had to. It was the times.'"

"The martial-arts and weapons part of the counterculture" was how another longtime SCA veteran described to me the way the organization was in the 1960s. It's hard to ignore, however, that the SCA does have an unhippie taste for rules and hierarchies. One section on the SCA's Web site (www.sca.org) is titled "What to Wear and How to Behave."

> Do not wear a white belt, sash or baldric (belt across the chest). White is reserved for members of the Chivalry. Bright colored belts, such as red, green, or yellow, are often used to indicate that the wearer is a student of a particular person who has been honored for excellence in an SCA field of endeavor. Although the colors are not restricted, in some kingdoms there may be a misunderstanding. Necklaces of chain links without medallions or pendants are also worn by special groups. You should avoid them until you ask about local customs.

The above passage sounds like the employee manual you would receive from HR on your first day as an Arthurian Knight in Medieval Land. It's a model for fun that takes as its inspiration the level of restraint and order you expect from the office. When I first encountered these rules I thought the level of order was there only to preserve the integrity of the escapist fantasy. But once I tracked down Darren, I realized that for some nerds the order is one of the main attractions, the escape itself.

## egalitarianism

Let's return to Jon L., who pointed out that my boffing stance made me look like I was taking a shit, fracturing the realness of our warrior-society fantasy world. In retrospect, Jon was only part of our group of boys because he had just moved from another town and was poor and we were the only ones who were nice to him. He lived with his mom in an equal-opportunity housing condo off Route 9, just over the border with Hadley, the tobacco farm town between Amherst and Northampton where developers had been allowed to build two malls, one now dying. He must have pretended to live in Amherst in order to go to our junior high. His mom had the kind of Massachusetts accent nobody in Amherst had. When I turned fourteen and sold my Nintendo and bought a guitar and grew my hair out and stopped boffing and started silk-screening the names of bands onto my T-shirts in art class, Jon L. became a leper to me.

The redeeming feature of the swordplay nerd "society" that the SCA embodies is that it demands courtesy and respect for rules but little else. When I was a thirteen-year-old boffer, I hung out with Jon L. and didn't care that he was more plainspoken than most of my classmates. That aspect of Jon L. didn't interest me much; the medieval landscape in my head was what I wanted, and if he could play some part in it he was okay by me. When I was a fourteen-year-old aspiring hipster I felt contaminated by him.

In the wild and idiotic delusions I experienced in my nerd phase, we were aristocrats, the Amherst boffers. But in reality we were among the least aristocratic kids in the whole school; anyone could join.

Similarly, the boffers in the SCA are outwardly aristocratic but actually egalitarian. You advance in status largely by acquiring skills and doing jobs. Under the aegis of the SCA, participants study agriculture, lace making, masonry, falconry, dyeing, bookmaking, bow making. Officers of each kingdom include the Seneschal (chief administration officer), the Pursuivant ("In charge of making announcements and helping people research their names and heraldic devices in preparation for submission to the College of Heralds"), a Knight Marshall (in charge of fighting), Chancellor of the Exchequer (treasurer), Minister of Arts ("coordinates the study and practice of the medieval arts and sciences"), and Chronicler, who edits the kingdom's newsletter.

Now, the mock violence in the SCA is integral to its system. This is not a pacifist fantasy of the Middle Ages. The king and queen of each kingdom come to power through winning a fighting tournament—they are "chosen by tournament combat"—and having been a king or queen at some point or at least being friends with one is necessary for establishing oneself in the peerage. A duke or duchess has been king or queen twice and must be addressed as "Your Grace." No effete Louis XIV business here; your rank is determined by your aptitude with a stick.

What, then, do the Middle Ages really represent to members of the SCA, if they can be meritocratic and still be the Middle Ages?

In a 1996 intro to the SCA's Web site, Mistress Siobhan Medhbh O'Roarke explained the Middle Ages this way:

> A feudal society takes its form from the idea of service and duty. A noble owes duty of service to his lord, who might be a Baron or Knight. In return, his lord owes protection from danger, and food, money, etc., in times of hardship. It is something like the idea of a pyramid club, but the benefits are greater and the idea of personal honor and mutual responsibility, not profit, tie the structure together (or at least it did in Europe for nearly a thousand years).

The feudal world of the SCA, then, is designed to be something like a corporation where the rules of meritocracy are followed more punctiliously than they are in real life. In the medieval period swordplay nerds have discovered a world of modern order, sanitation, and safety with a greater focus on courtesy, a more uniform dress code, and a class system that gives everybody a shot at the upper reaches of nobility. It's a different kind of Utopia from the one the hippies envisioned, in that instead of creating a loose tribe of individuals it creates a clearly defined social pyramid where upward mobility is a given but everybody follows the rules. Like the Masons, who convene in temples and reward ascent through a clearly defined hierarchy with sashes and rituals, the SCA provides a break from the *casualness* of postwar life. You don't need to be casual because everybody gets an opportunity to put on airs.

I was in fourth grade when I first observed that people who liked D&D—people like me—tended to be the *same ones* who liked to play with computers. Staggered by my first thrill of nationhood, I cast about for an explanation. It seemed to me what the two activities had in common is that they demand no physical prowess of any kind. Therefore the children like me who carried around the *Dungeon Master's Guide* and *How to Master LOGO* were distinguished by their intelligence. They didn't make time to exercise their bodies because they were committed to the exercise of their brains.

Through eighth grade, I clung to the belief that intelligence was the quality that made somebody a nerd. This meant that as a matter of routine, smart people were oppressed by the dumb. I told any classmate who would listen in fifth grade that sports appealed to stupid people because they required almost no intelligence, and as a result, I was usually pulverized whenever the teacher prodded me onto the dodge ball court. ("Get Ben out!" children would chant, in stoning formation.) The point at which I became irreversibly despised was when in response to this treatment I bunny-hopped backward out of bounds and shouted, "I quit! I quit!"

I had increasingly baroque fantasies about organized nerd societies that brooked no offense from the outside world. In junior high I envisioned a group of kids my age who wore black military uniforms with gold trim. There was a salute, a bottomless devotion to order and manners, and a standard in grooming at odds with the facts of my own appearance. When I had a crush on a girl, I would incorporate her into the largely male membership of my imaginary club, and I remember the way I shook hands in my mind with one such girl, her brown eyes gleaming beneath her black Oliver North cap, her smile as white as the flesh of an almond. At the time I thought the fantasy was asexual. I don't know what I thought we were all supposed to be doing, the nerds in uniform, but a mysterious activity brought us together that involved rules and skills uniquely our own. We were Harry Potter and the Third Reich.

I realize now that my fantasy resembled a traditional high-school popular crowd, with an ill-defined notion of intelligence replacing sports as the excuse for the chumminess and uniforms. Nerds were to me what the Aryan race was to Hitler: a group destined to control the world through its superior natural capabilities. I knew that in my junior high I was on the bottom rung, and I wanted nerdiness to be a power that uplifted me.

## back to sherry turkle

D&D allowed my friends and me to live as a group of superheroes, to make our perceived superiority and group loyalty translate into weapons and magic; it translated our social alienation into a physically treacherous landscape full of monsters. But there's another reason nerds like D&D. D&D is a game of pretend structured like a computer program, and people enjoy it in some of the same ways they enjoy computers. In the early 1980s, Sherry Turkle became intrigued by the cover of a book called *Principles of Compiler Design* that showed a knight on a horse fighting a dragon with a lance— weapon, steed, foe, and hero each labeled as metaphors for different programming entities. When she showed it to her students who were computer-science majors, they said, "Oh sure, a lot of compiler people are into D&D."

In Dungeons & Dragons, the player appointed Dungeon Master designs an "adventure" that is a kind of decision tree the other players must navigate. One MIT Dungeon Master whom Turkle observed devoted "at least five hours of preparation for each hour of play," throwing himself into his adventures to such an extent that he created "a social world structured like a machine."

Drawing on a skill set I developed at age eight, I will now create the beginning of a sample D&D adventure, to show what we're talking about here:

> *The characters begin in the town of Norsgall. The commercial shop of interest in the Norsgall center, abutting Mezgorath Square, is a smithy selling two recently forged weapons: a broadsword with a reach level of 5 that inflicts damage at a level of +2, and an ax modeled on the Maglish dwarf axes of Samidor, which has a reach level of only 3 but inflicts damage at a level of +4. The broadsword costs 14 gold pieces, the ax 16.*
>
> *Assuming the characters exit via the northern gates of Norsgall, they will encounter a fork in the road, with an eastern path into the mountains and a western path.*
>
> *If they choose the western path, they will encounter the following:*
>
> *1) Half a mile from Norsgall, an earth troll.*
>
> *The troll's stats are as follows:*
>
> *Dexterity: 16*
>
> *Strength: 18*
>
> *Intelligence: 12*
>
> *Wisdom: 14*

And so on. In writing an adventure, the Dungeon Master becomes a sci-fi author, thinking about the same issues the guys at LASFS were thinking about when they discussed dragon-on-dragon vs. dragon-on-man combat. The adventure would proceed to outline the different choices the characters could make at each juncture, and the frameworks for each challenge they faced. How the players' characters fare in combat depends both on the choices the players make—what equipment to buy, when to use which weapons and tools—and luck, the numbers that come up when they roll the dice. (D&D demands that players purchase a large variety of these at specialty stores, from the traditional six-sided, cubical die, to the Epcot-center-like, twenty-six-sided die).

Choice A will produce outcome X, which demands a randomly generated number according to process C that will create conclusion one, two, or three. Turkle observes this is more like creating a computer program (for the Dungeon Master) and using a computer program (for the non–Dungeon Master players) than it is a traditional game of make-believe, what she calls "You play the mommy and I play the daddy." In Mommy and Daddy, the roles can assume any shape, the players can behave with total unpredictability. The game consists of improvising a personality and understanding the personality improvised by the other player or players—the skill it demands is empathy. The rules can change as you go. If the players happen to develop a system of rules—and they don't have to—those rules can shift constantly. Conversely, in a computer program or a D&D adventure, a particular input will be subject to a set process and generate one of a limited number of outputs—which one depends on numbers randomly generated by dice or the computer. Football is a strategy game, too, but a football strategy can only generate a particular outcome when it's augmented with physical ability, and even the most skilled player must accept a high level of chaos and unpredictability when he lays down a plan. This, more than the crunching of shoulder bones against cleats and helmets, is what makes football un-nerdy.

## release

With puberty there generally arrived among my friends an interest in creating characters of the opposite sex, sometimes augmenting the statistical portraits (Strength: 17, Wisdom: 14) with seminude drawings, the shading so thoroughly cross-hatched that ball-point pens would die in the rendering of cleavage. The mathematical structure at the heart of it all made such self-expression seem tangential to the real business at hand: fighting monsters and conquering new lands by plugging numbers into formulas. Of course, as we fell deeper into manhood, the seminude drawing became kind of the whole point. As much as we liked rules, the rules became more and more an excuse for swinging a lantern over the frightening new monster in each person's head.

# case study:
# kenneth the demonslayer

I was a nerdy kid, but I had nothing on Kenneth. I knew this as soon as I laid eyes on the skeletal wrists sticking out of a polyblend sweatshirt, the frightened, near-laughing smile. I feel bad saying so, because it's clear to me now that Kenneth was one best friend I never should have bailed on; that is, the last thing he needed was for his best friend to bail. But then, like Darren, he couldn't tell me the bad things that were going on at the time. We had the vocabulary to deal with monsters, not humans.

Kenneth was in Mrs. Turner's sixth grade in Quad H at Wildwood Elementary in Amherst, the smallest boy in our class, with white skin, dark brown hair, and constantly moving fingers. He wore rayon blend sweatpants-sweatshirt combos from TJ Maxx just like mine, but they hung on him like you see them hanging on undernourished third-world child soldiers. Neither of us was surprised to find the other was into drawing elves with bo-staffs.

Kenneth and I used to play Apple IIe and Nintendo in the

basement of my neighbor Jonah's house. Jonah was a kid who liked to stand with his legs spread and his arms crossed, and he had a "Burn the Malls" pin he inherited from his older sister. One day the kids who were good at dodgeball kept bouncing the ball off Jonah's butt and calling him Fat-Ass Jonah, because he was thin but his butt was wide, so it was a perfectly framed target. Not long after that, Kenneth and I were playing Jonah at RBI Baseball on his Nintendo, and Jonah reached over and unplugged my controller.

I was quiet at first, and then he did it again, scoring four home runs. When I started crying, Jonah grabbed the blanket he'd been sitting on, pulled it over my head, knocked me down, and sat on me.

He hit me through the blanket. I couldn't see, and in my imagination, I was being murdered, smothered by a locally famous, maverick fat ass, through a scratchy blanket that lived in the basement and had dog hair in it, the worst way to die I had ever heard of. Suddenly, the blanket lifted, and I remember Kenneth actually looking like one of those skinny child combatants you see in the Middle East these days, throwing himself at Jonah and dragging him off. I ran away, hurling curses over my shoulder at Jonah, vowing to permanently sever our friendship, and Kenneth followed me back to my house.

"I realized I had to choose," says Kenneth, when I interview him now, eating a bowl of cereal in his kitchen near Boston. "And I, thought: Well, Jonah is an asshole. And I went with you."

Jonah had the better facilities; there was no Nintendo at my mom's house. But Kenneth went with the guy under the blanket instead of the guy over the blanket. It was that choice that made us best friends.

Kenneth bought something called ElfQuest: The Game at the mall comic store, and we'd play it for hours and only come out to pee. We'd look at the naked elf women in the *ElfQuest* comic book together. And when my dad once actually *spat on* the board of ElfQuest: The Game (which featured seminude elves in the graphics that lined the borders) we laughed at him. At that moment (for the first time?) we cared about each other's opinion more than we did our parents'.

This was a big deal, because Kenneth's mom had some heavy opinions.

Driving me home one night, with Kenneth beside me in the backseat, she began the questioning.

"Do you believe in ghosts and fairies, Ben?"

"No."

"I do. I believe in them because the Bible says they're real."

It was a summer night. Summers in the Pioneer Valley were known for thick pollen, ticklish air. Kenneth and I gazed out opposite windows, our bodies turned from each other.

"Ben, do you know what the Book of Mormon is?"

"I believe I am familiar with it."

"Do you know the Church of Latter-Day Saints?"

"I have seen the commercials."

She nodded, calmly, and I sensed we had arrived at a fragile but mutually satisfactory arrangement.

Kenneth's apartment struck me as an attractively Nintendo-friendly place; we could play for eons without somebody droning on about fresh air and nature, like people did at my house. But there were drawbacks I didn't know about. I didn't know that Kenneth's mom—Joanna—could take Kenneth and his little sister Hillary in her arms and coo to them, and call them her darlings, and ten minutes later walk into their rooms and begin to destroy their possessions, calling them the works of Satan. I didn't know that she could smack them both more or less at random; more relevant to my own situation, I didn't know that because of all this Kenneth had been defending people weaker than himself since he was a small child.

Joanna was one of the many Pioneer Valley former-hippie single mothers who'd found God. She'd grown up Catholic in a small industrial town. She'd met Kenneth's father, a Bostonian, in the last months of the hippie era, while he was hitchhiking across the country and just after she had left her first husband. They'd returned to Massachusetts a couple, and Kenneth was born in 1976 in Northampton, a city still at the beginning of a long climb toward prosperity. One day Mormon missionaries came to the household, a tiny rented cabin in Northampton's outlying woods, and his mother knew she had found her religion. Kenneth had just turned one.

The missionaries told Kenneth's father that if he reached the highest of the three levels of Mormon heaven, the Celestial Kingdom, he would be given his own planet over which he would reign as God. Pleased, he replied that he would create a planet that was all wilderness save for an excellent highway system and one motorcycle, which would be his, and that the human population would consist entirely of naked beautiful women who wanted to sleep with him. The missionaries explained that this was not quite in the spirit of things. You had to be a holier kind of god. Discouraged, he tolerated church, took Wonder Bread and water as sacrament, repressed his Tourette's syndrome, wore a blue jacket and red tie, and abstained from cigarettes, caffeine, and alcohol. He did these things because he loved Kenneth's mother, he would later tell Kenneth. It was clear she had found her place.

Kenneth's father left the church after Joanna extracted an indication from a bishop that the church did not want her to suck her husband's penis. When she threw him out of the house soon afterward, he knelt beside Kenneth and informed him of his new position in life.

"You're the man of the household," he said. "You have to take care of your mother and your sister, now."

It became clear Kenneth wasn't going to have to compete with his mother for the job.

"My mother is one of the few women I know who is not a feminist," Kenneth tells me today. "She believes that a woman can't hold down a job as well as a man, can't support a family as well as a man."

Soon they were broke.

Kenneth's new duty as a man first came into play when his mother broke a dish. She stared down at the pieces, and her mouth fell open, silently; Kenneth saw her and knew she was possessed by what the church called the Adversary. First he stood between her and Hillary. Then, in accordance with what he'd been taught in Sunday school, he went into the next room, dropped to his knees, and prayed to God to protect his mother from Lucifer's powers. He came back to the kitchen and told her what he'd done.

"Good, Kenneth," she said, quieted. "That's what you're supposed to do."

It was soon thereafter that Kenneth saw *The Empire Strikes Back* and fell in love with the AT-ATs, the four-legged land invasion vehicles with which Darth Vader assaults the rebel base on Ice Planet Hoth. When he and his mother got home from the theater, he sat on the foam pad on her floor where he slept and thought about them.

"I hope I get an AT-AT for Christmas," he said, lost in a holiday-season fantasy, and at this his mother stared at him and raised her hand. He understood from her face that he had made an error. Before he understood the significance of the motion he was struck and spinning backward.

Nobody knew it at the time, but this first indication of *Star Wars* fandom was, it appears, the start of a long, punishing struggle between Kenneth's mother and Kenneth's nerdiness.

She wasn't a big woman, but by the time I knew Kenneth she was still bigger than he was, and could still get rough when she got angry. I didn't know any of this. All I knew was that to be in the good graces of Joanna was to bask in an unusually intense glow of affection.

I sucked up to her, and sometimes I was good at it. When Kenneth started taking karate at the same dojo I did, she would come to pick us up and we'd each choose a soda from the soda machine. Kenneth would choose Coke. I would choose Slice, and turn the logo on the can toward Joanna as we walked toward her car, to make sure she could see I'd chosen caffeine-free.

"Kenneth," she said once, "Ben is Jewish and he's a better Mormon than you."

"I just think it tastes just as good," I intoned. Kenneth sipped his Coke very slowly, and stared out the window, holding the can close to his chest with two small hands.

A home video shows the two of us side by side in matching white karate *ki*s and yellow belts, chopping the air in sync beside the maple, each strike punctuated with the sound we've learned in class, a sharp exhalation of breath: *tssst*. Beyond karate class, we would meet as often as possible midway between our two houses, walking by Jonah's, and I'd always think about the coordinated attack we could make on Jonah if he ever were to come out and we both happened to be in our *kis*, one of us grabbing him from behind in a headlock while the other kneed him in the face until he lay belly up, rolling around on his butt. We'd walk toward each other, down the wide aisle of Victorians, and when we'd see each other from far away I'd feel myself smile, and our walks were excessively bouncy walks in the same way, walks that some called "fag walks," each a mirror of the other's liabilities. On the way back to my house, I would talk about my theories of how Life Really Works.

I gave Kenneth sermons against organized religion, and they made him go silent and a little wild-eyed. He told me about God, and being a Mormon. The teachings of the particular LDS church he attended included a forewarning of apocalypse taking place around the year 2000 or 2010. It was going to be a battle between the forces of God and the forces of Satan; there was going to be a computer or financial body based in Germany—The Beast—and it was going to come to control the government of the United States. The government was going to try to brand every member of the population with an ultraviolet mark on the wrist, and all good Mormons were going to refuse to have it put upon them. The government was then going to come to their houses and attempt to take them into camps. Churchgoers were therefore encouraged to own guns, and to stow away a six-month supply of water, in preparation for the fight against the government.

"That's impossible," I said once, and treated him to a lecture on the subjectivity of all human experience, consisting of facts gleaned from my mom's psychology textbooks.

*Tsssst!* His fist came within an inch of my face, and he withdrew it fast, nervous but ready to fight. I looked at him—eyes wide, legs spread in a karate fighting stance—and decided to shut up.

The next time I called, his stepfather, Ned, picked up the phone and told me Kenneth was unavailable. This was a state Kenneth had never been in before. My mother called next, and had a conversation with Joanna with the door closed. She sat me down on my bed.

"Joanna says you've been saying things to Kenneth that depressed Kenneth."

I nodded, willing to concede whatever necessary. I decided to lay off the no-God talk, and within a week both our moms were ferrying us between my house near downtown Amherst and Kenneth's new place out in the woods.

Clearly this took some doing on both sides. I didn't know it, of course, but the truth was it wasn't just me that kept Kenneth coming back to our house.

"I loved your mom," he tells me now, stiff facial hair encircling his mouth, annoying the part of my brain that believes we are still thirteen. "Your mom taught me that there was another way to be. She looked at problems rationally."

He figured this out one day when he mentioned to my mother that Joanna was afraid of Dungeons & Dragons. "She didn't want me playing D&D because it was the devil game, and there were always these kids getting into devil worship from it, and I remember your mom being like, 'No. That was one kid who had other mental problems.'" There was an apocalypse lining up in Kenneth's head. On one side there was the quiet, orderly world of my mother's house, and D&D and computer games; on the other there was his own stormier mother and her god.

By then, Kenneth, like many twelve-year-old Mormon males, had attained the rank of priest in the church, and could bless things and perform other functions a woman often could not; this allowed him new leeway with Joanna. "God's telling me it's okay," he would say when he wanted to borrow my old bicycle. "No, it's the devil talking to you!" she would say, in her musical girlish voice.

By this time she'd developed her own new weapon, pulling Kenneth out of Wildwood Elementary just before the end of sixth grade to homeschool him. I never saw what happened in the living room where the schooling took place, so I would ask Joanna in tones I believed to be neutral about her English and phys ed curricula, drinking a Slice in her living room with the Teenage Mutant Ninja Turtles & Other Strangeness manual under my arm.

She would answer in her ethereal cadences, silk tied to a table fan. "I wanted Kenneth and Hillary to have an education in the Book of Mormon *and* an education in the things you learn in school."

"Homeschooling with my mom is watching *Law & Order*," he tells me, years later. "She just keeps you in the house."

Today, I ask Kenneth what finally made him break with his mother and join the enemy. "It was all about having rules and control," he tells me now. He looks off into the entertainment area of his living room, where we are talking now, with a tincture of ambivalence around his eyes. "I idealized rules."

The battle that tipped the balance in favor of the world of D&D and computers, the outside world, and against Joanna, came on his fifteenth birthday, when his father showed up at the house with a stack of *Playboy*s and took him for a ride. He hadn't visited before, he explained to Kenneth, because he had already been inside once for a weed bust, and he was worried Joanna would have him thrown behind bars for failure to pay child support. He took him to meet his brother, an English teacher at Amherst Regional High School who taught Bible and Related Literature in a fashion that would not be permitted in a less liberal small town; he was famous among students for referring to himself as an "old faggot."

Kenneth's uncle, with his white beard, large glasses, and short-sleeved button-downs, was a great and sweaty teacher; my clearest memory of his instruction is when, unpacking Hawthorne's "Rappaccini's Daughter," he asked if anyone could guess what the Latin *rapio* meant, and when the extremely PC set of Amherst teenagers in that room declined to say the word, descended upon a free desk chair, drew it up toward his torso, and shouted "To seize!" He knew about Joanna's beliefs, and offered Kenneth a secular place to crash.

Pretty soon after that, it came to fists. One day Joanna began to hit Kenneth, and he used a wrist block he had practiced thousands of times in karate to stop her arm.

"I broke all the blood vessels in her wrist, pretty much."

He had always been so small, and now the physical dynamic was reversed.

"I saw her standing there with her back turned to me on the stairs," he says in his apartment now. "And I thought, 'I could kill her if I wanted,' and then I thought, 'Well, time to leave the house.' And I did."

He was fifteen. They never lived together again.

Maybe what Kenneth's mother found in her version of the

Church of Jesus Christ of Latter-Day Saints was to some extent the same thing we found in D&D. As haunted a woman as she was, without her guidebooks, as it were, the promise of power in a celestial home, she might have been worse. What the missionaries who converted her offered was a planet where she was God. Her sex wasn't meant for worldly success, but one day she would be a Dungeon Master, very far away.

I remember World Builder, a program Kenneth and I used to play with for hours on my own mother's Macintosh. You created a series of imaginary landscapes and monsters that all your friends could then navigate, making yes or no choices; it was primitive game design. Nobody ever wanted to come over and experience one of the static black-and-white worlds Kenneth and I built, but we loved World Builder regardless because we liked being gods. Another name for World Builder, it occurs to me now, is You Get Your Own Planet.

Kenneth got a scholarship to a boarding school an hour away and moved into the dormitory, then later to his uncle's house. The boarding school gave him two awards for his near-military adherence to its codes of behavior, and he expanded his repertoire of martial arts, taking up saber fencing, and new forms of hand-to-hand combat, defenses against knives becoming a specialty. In my last memory of Kenneth from our boyhoods, the last time we hung out before I broke off contact with him completely, his uncle pulls up beside us in his old American car to drive him back to Shutesbury. "Hello, hoodlums," he calls out, in his dignified Katharine Hepburn way. Kenneth climbs in next to him, and the engine scatters dry brown leaves.

The next time I see Kenneth we are in his living room fifteen years later.

He tells me how he scored enough financial aid to go to college, where he befriended an assortment of gamers and pot smokers and intellectuals, starting smoking cigarettes, did the occasional hit of acid, met his fiancée. One night he noticed something.

"In college we played a lot of Warhammer, the role-playing game, and I remember looking around this table of twelve of my friends, and I remember getting frustrated because people weren't playing it as a game. It was all like, 'That's how my character *feels,* man, there's nothing I can do about it.' But people's characters were just projections of who they wanted to be. No matter what game we played the character never really changed.

"My guy was always big," recalls Kenneth. "I never made my guy smart. He was always the huge fighter with really high strength. Because when I was a kid my thing was that I was smart, but I was short."

This is true. When we played D&D together, just the two of us, he was Kenneth the Demonslayer, invariably depicted in blue pen drawings as having a bull's deltoids and a thimble head.

"I loved playing him, man, I loved it, it was so imbalanced I would keep losing limbs and keep getting Mithril[1] limbs, it was this indestructible metal, and I just envisioned that guy as me only stronger."

When he looked at his friends, he saw them acting out fantasies the way he had when he was thirteen. He came up with a word for the practice: "self-construction."

"One guy always wanted to be the party leader but he was a ter-

---

1. A light, silvery, virtually indestructible metal in *The Lord of the Rings,* often used to make armor; MIThril is, for this reason, the name of an MIT research group that designs computer-enhanced clothing.

rible leader, and another guy wanted to be the really sly business-savvy guy, and I always wanted to be big."

From that time onward he found gaming was too reminiscent of bad acting to be enjoyable; everybody was playing a part to create a myth of themselves they needed. Every performance conveyed not the magic powers of the character but the neediness of the performer ("I am a Frost Giant!"). The nerdy activities might partly replace religion but they couldn't compete with religion's claim to be real.

He learned fencing, and new forms of karate, then stick-fighting, which he loved the best. A year after graduation, he visited his father in a hospice as he died of spine and lung cancer. A few years after that he found his first good job, as a game tester at the Boston company that developed video games, and worked his way up into a management position.

"If everything goes according to plan," he says now, "I should have a house in two years."

He oversees a department of twenty-odd game testers, most of them aged nineteen to twenty-six, monitoring productivity, hiring and firing, working long hours in the summer ironing out the bugs on titles due out Black Friday. "I used to have ambitions to design games," he says, "because of that Super Mario Bros. 2 Role-Playing Game I made you."

His eyebrows jump at the recognition and surprise in my face.

"Remember that sheaf of papers?" he asks, his expression philosophical.

Suddenly I do. A set of charts and illustrations photocopied from faint pen marks, thirty or so pages long, a picture of Mario on the front, in mid-leap, holding an anthropomorphic turnip.

"We were broke and I panicked," he reveals. "Your birthday was coming up and I didn't know what to get you and I considered you my best friend. So I spent a week on it."

I realize that for having abandoned this friend I am going to hell.

At any rate, nerdiness won and became Kenneth's livelihood; Joanna lost.

"My mother's been married six times now," he says. "The last one lasted twelve hours. She met this guy at a Mormon elders' singles mixer, and married him there, at the mixer, and went back to his house and spent the night with him. Then she woke up and realized this guy was really poor and divorced him. Plus she goes in for pyramid scheme after pyramid scheme. Right now it's this juice from Australia. She calls me up and says"—his voice floats up into an impersonation of the breathy tones I still remember— "'Kenneth, it cures AIDS, and it cures cancer, it's the most wonderful thing.'

"I don't love my mother," he tells me, looking away. Then he looks me in the eye and repeats it. "People don't believe me, but I don't."

"Hillary's still part of the Mormon church. She has kids now, and she lives near my mom. Married to a nice guy. My brother Danny's a good kid. He's nineteen, and he's been homeschooled by my mom his entire life, so social interaction isn't really something he learned. All he really learned is from my mom. They live together. They're both on state welfare."

The love of rules hasn't flagged, really. "It used to be that if I noticed my fiancée had moved one of the tuna cans from where I put it on the shelf I freaked out. Now I take meds for bipolar disorder, and they're awesome. I still get the feeling of, 'Aaaah the tuna can is

on a different shelf!' and it's the exact same feeling, but now it's behind a wall."

"It's funny," he says a little later. "I'll look pretty silly if I try to play
volleyball, but I'm confident I could kill a person with my bare
hands. That childhood of violence, not just my mother but the
church, the stuff we learned; it's still with me. When I walk the dog
at night, I carry an umbrella in my back pocket when it's not rain-
ing. My fiancée won't let me own a gun, but I still sleep with my
stick next to my bed."

He looks at the piles of gaming material that run along two of
his walls.

"And I still play a lot of Worlds of Warcraft because that's where
my friends are; we talk on the headsets."

His small, trembling, slightly squirrel-like, off-white mutt begins to point itself toward the door to indicate it needs a walk.

"And I don't play with my Magic cards anymore," he adds, in
measured tones, "but I do take them out and organize them."

We go outside and say our good-byes, lingering, suddenly aware
of how much older we are than the last time we parted. I'm almost
thirty now; he's thirty-one. Our hairlines have receded by the same
amount. He walks the excitable squirrel-mutt, which he informs
me was rescued from a nearby house of cocaine addicts who used
to shut it in a closet. It noses the ground obsessively, accounting for
every speck of dust, until it's finally pulled away. I think about
death; that is, I think about how little time we get and how much
time we spend inventing and following rules that make us feel immortal and safe.

It's dumb, I know, to engage in one of those self-aggrandizing dialogues with a great author like E. M. Forster. But still. When I think about Kenneth I think about the observation in *Howards End* that Tibby is a person about whom little need be premised, that nerdy young men, basically, are too simple to squander the reader's time on, and I shake my impotent twenty-first-century fist and go, *E.M., are you kidding me?*

But let's return to why I ditched my nerdy friends.

*part 3*

# my credentials

As a boy I craved safety more than I craved affection. Other children tried to get some kind of reaction out of me until I talked to them, and when I tried to push them away, they bounced back angrier.

It would go like this:

*Girl (two grades younger than me, on school bus): Ben, you're gay.*
*Everyone can kick your ass. You are such a faggot. Look at you.*
*You can't even comb your hair, and your shirt isn't buttoned*
*right. You are so pathetic.*
*Me: You are an idiot.*
*Girl: Why am I an idiot?*
*Me: You like sports. Sports are for people who are stupid.*
*Girl: Sports aren't for people who are stupid.*
*Me: Yeah they are. It's always the people that are really stupid that*
*are good at sports.*
*Girl: That's not true.*

*Me: Yeah it is. Sports don't require any intelligence.*

*Girl: Hey, Ben just said sports don't require any intelligence and*
   *people who are good at sports are stupid.*

*Mob of children: Ben you are a racist faggot.*

I wanted to be like a machine and like a wizard. These seemed to me similar things. They were competent and emotionally blank. I liked video games because they were the way into the wizard/machine feeling.

The wizard/machine feeling came from being reliably rewarded for practicing, for the acquisition of expertise. In the wizard/machine feeling I was competent; in the wizard/machine feeling I didn't need to exhibit the sports combination of menace and jocularity. (Of course, the feeling of competence and progress and group loyalty was precisely what others found in sports.) There was no point in being intimidating in the flesh, because your expertise was funneled through your fingers into a different body on the screen. It was an out-of-body experience and a sensation of control.

As I write these words I'm on an Amtrak car shuddering through my hometown of Amherst, Massachusetts. It looks like an Edwardian suburb under thick snow, populated by pink-cheeked, bespectacled half-Jewish Vikings in hoodies. Well, I think, it's not like I grew up in America or anything. I was a nerd in the most self-consciously tolerant region of the continent. I must carry within me some crystalline nerd essence to have been despised so richly in Amherst.

I'm different from Kenneth and Darren in that I made an abrupt break with all nerdy activities midway through adolescence.

I was a big nerd, but I was a self-loathing nerd, and the story of my youth is a story of escape attempts.

## therapies,
## age five to six

1. I'm escorted to stand in place alone with Mr. Riordan, our gym teacher, on the basketball court, and learn how to dribble a basketball.

2. After an anxiety attack in which I refuse to ever play soccer again because I am afraid the ball will hit my head, I see a child psychologist named Bernie for weekly sessions. I eat M&Ms out of a glass duck in his office. In addition to the M&Ms, Bernie has many candy-coated nuts, which I devour in small mountain ranges. My favorite activity to do with Bernie, second to eating M&Ms out of his duck, is to describe my athletic achievements. I make football fields with green markers and rulers on his drawing paper, and arrange football players in flying wedges on the field to illustrate the tactics behind my touchdowns. I describe the fence of invisibility around the swimming pool where I do my laps.

"You know, when I was a kid I moved to a new school," Bernie says. "I was so scared of my new school that I told the teacher I could speak Chinese. It was very embarrassing for me afterward. But I was feeling scared, so I lied to make myself feel better." He never calls me on my lies in any more explicit way.

The next day, in second grade, I tell my friends I speak Chinese. They are excited. I translate any sentence they want with lightning speed, making Chinesey sounds. "This grape juice tastes like Isaac's mom's poop" is easy, and elicits the most praise.

While we're waiting for the school bus at the end of the day, an Asian-American kid our age is behind us in line.

"That kid's Chinese," the son of a liberal activist lawyer says to me. "Say something to him."

I turn to the kid and speak my Chinese. He looks off into the gray sky—it's the kind of day that makes our Luke Skywalker 1983 haircuts stick to our foreheads. It's a look I think I've had on my own face before: the plaintive, skeptical eyebrows that ask, When is it going to stop?

Maybe Mom needs to fire my therapist, I think to myself, this isn't actually my fault. But of course what has happened is an instance—the first instance—of my fantasy life damaging my real life. An escapist, alternate existence that impacts other people in the real world, and moves me to seek only the company of those who would allow me to sustain it. In short, a fantasy addiction. This is the mark of a certain kind of nerd.

3. After school, in my youth soccer league, the coach takes me aside. "If you're not the best soccer player in the world, you can just kind of stand in front of somebody on the other team and keep him from moving the ball," he explains.

We practice standing in front of people. Despair.

## therapies,
## age eight

My parents hire Jean, a physical therapist, for a special session, to teach me to ride a bike without training wheels. Several times, I topple into the mud by the side of the road and the lesson becomes a Vietnam tableaux, with me crying hysterically in my attempt to extricate myself from the vehicle and Jean guiding my body gingerly from the mire and wreckage. A few months later, I make an announcement.

"Why don't I just get my Swiss Army knife and kill myself?" I say. I run upstairs to my room and get my Swiss Army knife out of the drawer. I almost have the blade out when my mom runs upstairs, takes it from me, and drags me into her room to talk.

"You need help," she says.

"Don't put me in a mental hospital," I say. "Please don't put me in the mental hospital." I'm crying.

"What do we do in this family when somebody needs help?"

My imagination runs wild, and then suddenly things become clear. "We're going to go see Bernie," I say, realizing it as I say it.

We walk into Bernie's office together, and I plunge my hand into the glass duck. The M&Ms swallow my hand. Bernie listens carefully, wrinkling his brow in concentration. But as I sit in his office and dutifully report what occurred, I cry harder than I did in my mother's room when I begged not to be institutionalized. The delusion that allowed me to believe Bernie never doubted my portrait of myself as a star athlete is melting away. Clearly a boy who tries, ineptly, to stab himself in the heart with a device intended for cutting cheese on a picnic is not a boy who excels at football. There's nobody left in the world who can be deceived, and the fantasy existence of Ben Nugent the football star shrinks away. It is my first experience of being dragged away from a fantasy.

## age nine

My parents split up, and Jonah and his friend use me as a starting point for a discussion on the negative effects of divorce upon children. At our cafeteria table at lunch, they put on skits in which they play my mother and father.

*Jonah: Ben's an imbecile.*
*Nick: No, Ben's a gay retard.*
*Jonah: Fuck you, we're getting a divorce.*

I learn that real life is not something you should talk about with your friends. From this point onward, our mode of connection will be Dungeons & Dragons, the Nintendo, and the Apple IIe. So begins the age of the oak table at the Jones Library. My father buys me a Nintendo, and I am only allowed to use it at his house, where I live on weekends. I play it for about half of the day and most of the night.

## age thirteen

There's some kind of mental deformity afflicting my generation that drives us to Eastern Europe for our coming-of-age experiences. In my third year of Russian, in ninth grade, I spend three weeks with a family in Petrozavodsk, a small Karelian city a couple of hundred miles from the Arctic Circle, and make dogged attempts at cross-cultural togetherness. Then a group of kids from my high school goes to Moscow for three days. I'm in my room in our hotel, at the Soviet-era Hotel 6–like desk with a little Hotel 6–like lamp, when fate knocks, in the form of Ashley, Seth, and Scott, who are, by Russian Club standards, quite popular.

Scott hands me a bottle of peach liqueur.

"I'm not into drinking," I say. A minute later, a post-Soviet Dixie cup of dull orange liquid is buckling against my lip. This paragraph, I realize, looks like it belongs in a substance-abuse memoir, so I'll go with it—it's the most luscious, natural peach flavor in the whole world. They pull me into the room where all fifteen members of the group have piled together. It's warm and dark—not every Hotel 6 lamp that could be lit has been lit. We are like astronauts in an escape pod that has detached. I feel I would protect these people with my life. Girls laugh and touch my shoulder, because it is funny I am drunk. I decide I would kill any man who offended them. The normal rules don't apply; the social order does not assert itself. I am not ridiculed. We are drunk, and for one ridiculous moment nobody is focused on the fact that I am hideous and awkward, if only because I now register as *Ben: thirteen-year-old male, in love and trashed to the point of loss of reason*, instead of *Ben: thirteen-year-old male, nerd*. Once I know what it is to be the former, I can't go back.

I am generally able to squeeze through the academic trials of Amherst Regional High School Russian, which function as a filter for membership in the Russian Club's inner circle, forcing the less dedicated acolytes to take up a different language. The second semester of ninth grade, our teacher asks us to read Tolstoy's "Master and Man" in the original Russian, then write a three-page opinion paper on it in the same language. I read the second page of

"Khozyain i Rabotnik" over and over again, and never get halfway down.

These are the things I write about in the Cyrillic font on the Mac Classic:

> *Tolstoy having sex with a girl in my Russian class.*
> *Tolstoy having sex with my teacher.*
> *Tolstoy having sex with the sister of the girl in my Russian class.*
> *The lyrics of The Byrds.*

This is a filibuster, a means of filling up pages so that I can show my mother rows of Cyrillic letters and she will be satisfied that progress is being made. The last night before the paper is due, I plan to read the story and write the paper in an epic all-nighter. Because this doesn't happen, and because my mother strictly monitors the progress, checking to make sure I produce new paragraphs on schedule, finally I have no choice but to print out the nonsensical writing, show it to her (she can't read Russian), and take it to school.

Because I've written my paper on my computer, everybody pauses to admire my little manuscript. The girl who is extensively described as having intercourse with Tolstoy, along with her sister, pauses over it, and hands it back to me wordlessly before I take it up to the teacher's desk.

My teacher calls our house the same night, and asks my mother to put me on the phone.

"So what happened with your paper?" she asks.

"What do you mean?" I stammer. "Is there something wrong?"

I feel a familiar sensation building in my stomach, and after a moment of silence on the other end of the line, I know what it is: the feeling of having to maintain that I spoke Chinese so badly that

I made Chinesey sounds at an Asian kid. Of allowing a fantasy to become more and more important until it rises from the table, like Frankenstein's creature, and stalks around the real world, spilling the blood of innocents.

"Well, I can't imagine what happened," I hear myself saying. "You know, one possibility is there's a couple of my friends who take Russian, like Darren, who were fooling around with my computer the other day."

Everybody knows Darren comes from the Ghetto of Amherst, I think to myself. They will believe he did this. Everyone will believe he is "troubled" and forgive him.

By now, Darren's mother has told him that his biological father is not the father he knows. His black "father" was the man his mother met after she broke up with the Puerto Rican whose genetic material was actually his. He, Darren, had always been lied to about it. Our black Dungeon Master, the black kids' Mr. Wannabe White Guy, is half-Englishman, half-Latino. Motown, black slang from the eighties, these things still evoke memories of childhood for Darren. His blackness is like his Normal Family, once fully possessed, then debunked, now gone. But we don't know this. We know him as the Black Kid Who Takes Russian.

I use the Darren story on my mother as well as my teacher. "Oh, boy," my mother says, "he comes from a rough place." So far as I can tell, adults are quietly stepping away from the matter, if not with belief, then with sufficient ambivalence as to provide space to wiggle free.

Then I walk my poodle with Kenneth, who is sleeping over.

"Man, Darren is one fucked-up kid," Kenneth says.

"I wrote it," I say. It is a May night. In the lamplight, we turn away from my poodle, Sparky, so that he feels comfortable pooping on the outer limits of the neighbor's grass, and watch the bugs cover our T-shirts ("Moscow" in Cyrillic on mine; an old "Cowabunga!" on Kenneth's).

"What do you mean?" he asks.

"I wrote the Russian essay," I say. "You can't tell anybody."

He nods, his voice and eyebrows emphasizing the last three words: "You and I are really good friends."

I see both Kenneth and Darren less and less. I believe it is their inability to *understand my newly artistic point of view,* and because Kenneth moves to Greenfield and Darren moves to Belchertown, each half an hour away in different directions. But of course it is also because of the Russian essay. Darren is the one I betrayed and Kenneth is the one who knows. I become one of those high-school shape-shifters, drama kid, hippie kid, pretentious jazz guy. I will hang out with anyone but the nerds.

"Hey, we're all going to our house after school to fuck shit up on Ninja Gaiden," says Darren one day, calling to me from a bench in the courtyard in front of Amherst Regional.

"That's okay," I say. "I'm not really into violent video games anymore these days."

He stares at me, and I stare back, as appalled by own words as they are. But there is no return.

## good-bye, nerd america

I remember many dust particles under the lamps in a dim oak living room of a Russian Club member's *Howards End*–era house as the sun went down, a state of anticipation, a change coming, a rich winter darkness blowing toward us. There was an album that played in the background as we squeezed frosting designs onto the Yeltsin Cake, which would feature in the Russian Club bake sale. As the album played, three girls two years my senior reacted in a way I had never seen them react to anything. There was a state of excitement, quietly conveyed, in the way they fidgeted with the blue booklet with the baby swimming on the cover, the way they would forget about the frosting tube they were strangling, in the middle of an important design element, and listen to a song. At the ends of the songs, the last guitar chord would hang in the air like an offered hand. The Yeltsin Cake was inordinately expressive in its use of color that year, and lacking in verisimilitude; we were hearing Nirvana's *Nevermind* for the first time.

A few months later, I lay my SuperNintendo in a cardboard box, surrounded by its game cartridges, like a mother pig with sucklings, and walk a mile through the snow to Jon L.'s, where I hand it over to Kenneth for five twenties. Jon watches and does a victory dance on Kenneth's behalf. He can't believe the extent to which I have gone crazy.


I don't see Darren for the next thirteen years. In the summer of 2007, after our interview, I deposit him by the Amherst Town Common, at the Episcopalian church in whose hall we once waited tables together at the Russian Club Vecherinka Celebration Dinner in matching Russian peasant doublets. For a moment, I think I am going to ask him if he knew that I falsely incriminated him when we were fourteen. We shake hands and wish each other good luck, and he leaves, never elated at my presence, never hostile, perfectly cooperative.

I watch him walk into the church offices, hands in pockets,

short-sleeved button-down shirt buttoned one button too high. It occurs to me that many people who have withstood arbitrary punishments from life are not tough, in any conventional sense of the word. They may hunger for order and escape, and button their shirts all the way, and love charts and computers. Sometimes they favor large, steely glasses that are hard to destroy.

# acknowledgments

Thank you, Amy Williams and Brant Rumble. You were the grandparents of this book when I was its barely competent single father. Hopefully, the next book will be an epic poem about the Baker women: Dora, Linda, Ellie, Annie. They were all indispensable for different reasons. My father, Conn, taught me how to think historically. Uncle Mark gave me a car, and Uncle Rory gave me a barn to write in at one point. Mel Flashman and Rachel and Gabe Reilich were my friends. Paul Feig, Anne Beatts, and Rosie Shuster were up for talking about their work, and the guys who grew up with me were up for talking about whatever I wanted.

# about the author

Benjamin Nugent has written for *The New York Times Magazine*, *Time*, *New York*, and *n+1*. He's Lead Blogger for Greenish, an on-line magazine about environmentalism. His first book, *Elliott Smith and the Big Nothing*, came out in 2004.